SURVIVING YOUR SPLIT

SURVIVING YOUR SPLIT

A guide to separation, divorce and family law in Australia

LUCY MANNERING
& REBEKAH MANNERING

MELBOURNE UNIVERSITY PRESS
An imprint of Melbourne University Publishing Limited
Level 1, 715 Swanston Street, Carlton, Victoria 3053, Australia
mup-contact@unimelb.edu.au
www.mup.com.au

First published 2018
Reprinted 2025

Cover design by Design by Committee
Typeset by Megan Ellis
Printed in Australia by McPherson's Printing Group

A catalogue record for this book is available from the National Library of Australia

9780522872781 (paperback)
9780522872798 (ebook)

Contents

Welcome to the club

Welcome to the club that you never wanted to join. When we stood in front of our family and friends and pledged until death do us part, we never thought we'd be among the 94 000 Australians who get divorced every year, and you probably didn't, either. Or maybe you did—maybe your divorce has been a long time coming. Maybe you're initiating it. Maybe your mum told you on your wedding day not to go through with it, like one bride we know. But then again, maybe it's come completely out of the blue.

Or perhaps your de facto relationship, with houses or assets, children or fur-babies, or a mix of all of them, has come to an end.

Whatever route you've taken to get here, you're splitting up. And it's a scary, confusing time. For most people, divorce is what psychologists like to call a 'major life crisis', and it comes in at number two on the list of Really Horrible Things That Can Happen To Humans, just behind the death of a spouse or a loved one.

And yes, there may be times when you truly believe that your spouse dying would have been easier than the hell you're going through now. If they were dead, you wouldn't be facing the prospect of possibly losing your home and time with your kids, not to mention the embarrassment of your marriage ending. Right now, divorce might seem like the worst thing in the world.

But we're here to say—you will get through this. We did. Rebekah separated from her first husband four months before Lucy separated from hers. And as lawyers, who grew up as the children of family lawyers, even *we* sometimes felt scared and confused as we navigated a strange new world that we never thought we'd be part of. We've also helped our friends with their separations and divorces, and we realised how valuable it is to have easy access to expert advice and support. We hope you'll see this book as the next best thing to having a family lawyer as your best friend.

We know how to find our way around the bureaucratic nightmare that is the family law system, and we know how to fill in form J(2) a(ii) in triplicate and what a section 60I certificate is, and where exactly to put the initials at the bottom of each page. We might not be awesome at first marriages, but this is about divorce, not staying married to your first partner (because at that, we again admit, we're not great).

So, given our experience both personal and professional in this field, we wrote this book. It's for everyone who wants some help navigating the legal minefield that divorce can be, and who is looking for some tips on how to get through it with their life relatively intact—and with an even better, happier life on the other side.

It's not anti-man or anti-woman, or anti-dads or anti-mums (we don't really want to limit our potential audience like that; we're not crazy, after all—we'll take all the money). Most of all, it's a book designed to help you through this difficult period in your life. Even the most toxic divorce is better than the alternative—staying in a toxic marriage.

We'll look at how you can survive, and thrive, during and after your divorce. The book is broken into sections covering the bits many people find the most difficult aspects of ending a relationship—like the first few days, the first month, the first Christmas, and the first night without your kids. We've included case studies to help put into context the issues we discuss—most are from cases we, or our colleagues, have worked on, but some are stories we've been told by friends and family.

We know lawyers are expensive. We know they can be difficult to talk to. We know they say annoying things like 'Well, the case of blah and blah said xyz,[1] but really it's hard to say what any given judge will decide on the day', when you just want *answers*, dammit!

1 When a law-talking person references case law (that's where the judge makes a decision) they don't pronounce the 'v.' as in 'versus'. So Potter v. Potter becomes Potter and Potter. But it's sometimes still written as 'v.'. There will be an extremely esoteric reason for why this is, and we bet it has something to do with feudal England. Most things in the common law (that's another term for judge-made law) are something to do with feudal England.

We know that you might not have any idea what's first, or what's next. This book isn't an alternative to getting the best family lawyer you can find. You must get yourself a lawyer if you can. If you have no access to funds, or you have low funds, we'll explain how to contact Legal Aid or another legal service assistance provider in your state. But what this book will do is help you understand the basics of the family law system, while saving you money by giving you the tools you'll need to navigate through it.

With our help, you'll be armed with the most up-to-date tips on getting the best outcome for you, and for your family, and how to do it without totally destroying your relationship with your former spouse. After all, they're not going anywhere (especially if you've got kids—then they're really, really not going anywhere) and you've got them in your life forever. Make it so you can look back on this stage of your life and say, 'I behaved well, and fairly, even though I was so angry that I looked up whether provocation was still a partial defence to murder in my state'.[2]

And although we're not psychologists (if you can, you should see an actual psychologist), we've included a bit about the psychology of divorce, and attachment theory, and how grief works, which can help explain why you feel so very awful, even if you want to get divorced.

The book also includes worksheets that you can use (if you're a worksheet kind of person) to help you make plans for your future, or to help you clarify in your mind what you really want, and to help you get a clear idea of questions you want to ask your lawyer.

Studies have shown that writing things down makes us much more likely to implement our plans, and helps us realise what we actually want to achieve, and what questions we need to ask. The vast majority of businesses have business plans, and the worksheets are a way of using these techniques to help you through this time.

And remember—marriages come and go, but divorce is forever!

2 Don't look this up.

Safety note

The sad truth is that the most dangerous time for a woman is when she is leaving a relationship. In 2015, eighty women were killed by their domestic partners in Australia.[3]

If you have *any* reason, or even if you only think you might have a reason, to fear your partner, male or female, there is help available by calling 1800 RESPECT.

A few statistics

According to the Australian Bureau of Statistics:

- There were 113 595 marriages and 46 517 divorces in Australia in 2015. (This doesn't of course include the many de facto partnerships that Australians entered into and left in that year, so the actual numbers are much higher.)
- Most marriages ended at the twelve-year mark.
- Most men got divorced at about age forty-five, while most women got divorced at about age forty-two.
- The end of a relationship where kids (under the age of eighteen) are involved accounted for 47.5 per cent of all divorces.
- Women initiate divorce proceedings more often than men but the majority of divorce applications are 'joint' (43.3 per cent).
- More and more marriages are ending around the twenty-year mark (an increase from 13 per cent in 1990 to 28 per cent in 2011).[4]
- And the average number of kids involved for each couple was 1.8.

---

3 Counting Dead Women, Destroy the Joint, @Destroythejoint.
4 Australian Institute of Family Studies—'Twenty Year Itch'—2013.

1

The first few days

The beginning of your journey

So let's start at the beginning. You've either had a bombshell dropped on you, or you've dropped your own. The relationship is over. You or your spouse, or perhaps both of you, want a divorce.

This is big, life-changing news. Sometimes it comes out during yet another (failed) marriage counselling session, or maybe you've been discussing it for a long time. Sometimes, one of you has had an 'exit affair' and they've lined up the next victim (joking! Just joking!) before you've even had the conversation.

Regardless of how you've come to the point where your marriage is over (and this time really over), the first few days are very important. Our mother always told us 'Start as you mean to go on', and so, if you can, start and finish with your dignity and your grace intact.

First things first—urgent matters

Some things just can't wait. The actions you take in the first few days post-separation can make the difference between a disastrous outcome and an outcome you can happily live with. Below, we have outlined some of the most difficult-to-unravel issues, and what you can do about them.

International parental abduction

One parent removing the children from the country they live in and permanently taking them to another country without the permission of the other parent (or the court) is rare but devastating, particularly if the abducting parent takes the children to a country that won't return them. If your ex has financial or relationship ties to another country and/or has made threats to take the children to another country, then you must get urgent legal advice from a family lawyer.

A PACE (Passenger Analysis, Clearance and Evacuation System) Alert, also known as the Airport Watchlist, lets police know if children on the watchlist are being taken out of Australia. The Australian Federal Police will stop the children from being taken onto an aircraft or ship.

If you believe that your child or children are going to be taken out of the country, then do not delay. There's nothing more heartbreaking than having a watchlist order made that misses the children leaving by an hour. If you cannot get in to see your family lawyer, the Australian Federal Police has comprehensive assistance on their website.[5] The family law courts can make urgent orders if necessary.

Some countries are signatories to the United Nations Hague Convention on the Civil Aspects of International Child Abduction and these countries are regularly updated on the Australian Attorney-General's Department site, at www.ag.gov.au. This convention means that parenting matters will be dealt with in a child's place of habitual residence, so children will usually be returned for the parenting matter to be worked out.

Non-Hague countries include India, Pakistan, Indonesia (including Bali), Malaysia, the People's Republic of China, Lebanon and the United Arab Emirates. These countries generally will not return children.

Don't surrender your children's passports to the other parent, or, if they haven't got passports, don't agree to them being issued passports, until you have sought urgent legal advice. Even if the country

5 www.afp.gov.au/what-we-do/crime-types/family-law-kit.

is a signatory to the Hague Convention, it can take time for children to be returned and it is a stressful process. (This is an understatement. It will probably be the worst thing you've ever gone through.)

If you think that your ex will ask the Passport Office to issue a passport for the children or if you think that passports will be reported stolen and reissued, you can lodge a Child Alert with the Australian Passport Office.[6] This lets the Passport Office know that they need to check with you before issuing a passport. Although there is a requirement for both parents to sign a passport application, it is not unknown for parents to forge the other parent's signature. Usually they are found out and prosecuted.

Self-managed superannuation funds and joint bank accounts

These can also be a source of serious problems.

We want to believe the best of people but sometimes they behave very badly. Money can go missing and bank accounts and self-managed super funds get raided, with devastating results (as in not only do you lose the cash, but you may actually also get fined and taxed).

You must let your bank know straight away, as soon as possible, that you have separated and ask that any joint accounts, including super accounts and term deposits, be changed so that two signatures are required to withdraw money or to set up direct debits. The bank can also flag your accounts so that you are notified of any attempts to remove money from your joint accounts.

You should try to reach an agreement (in writing, so via email or text message) with your now-ex about how money in the joint accounts can be spent in the early days of your separation—with an agreed daily limit and only on your ordinary expenses—like on your mortgage, school fees or child care, groceries and other bills that you would normally pay. This isn't the time for either of you to go on spending sprees! Be aware that if you don't close down your joint bank accounts post-separation, you will be liable for paying tax on any interest the account earns.

---

6 www.passports.gov.au/passportsexplained/childpassports/Pages/childalerts.aspx.

All this is especially important if you have a self-managed super fund that has cash or shares that are accessible, because they are still treated as super and you could be liable for tax and penalties even if your former spouse took the cash and moved to Turkey.[7]

To elaborate, if you are a trustee of the super fund with your ex, you could still be liable for their bad behaviour, particularly if they make off with the funds overseas.[8]

This was what happened in the case of Shail Superannuation Fund where the husband withdrew $3 460 000 from a cash management account owned by the self-managed super fund. The money was then transferred to an account in the husband's name in Turkey. While the Administrative Appeals Tribunal was sympathetic towards Mrs Shail, the law was the law and she was found to be just as liable as Mr Shail for the tax and penalty (which meant she had to pay some $1 583 873.68 in tax and $1 475 322.50 in penalties for not paying tax). If you have a self-managed superannuation fund, you *must* seek urgent legal advice as soon as possible.

> **Case**—when a person makes an application to a court for orders (that is, a decision of the court), that becomes the case before the court. It can also be called your 'matter', but generally only before it becomes a 'case'. We like to keep you on your toes.

Time limits apply in property and spousal maintenance cases. You usually need 'leave' (special permission that might not be given) of the court to make an application for property orders or spousal maintenance orders after the time limit is up. The time limits are:

- twelve months after the divorce order becomes final for couples that are/were married
- two years after separation for couples that were in a de facto relationship.

7 Shail Superannuation Fund and Commissioner of Taxation [2011] AATA 940 (23 December 2011), www.austlii.edu.au/au/cases/cth/AATA/2011/940.html.

8 www.austlii.edu.au/au/cases/cth/AATA/2011/940.html.

Leave will only be granted if:

- hardship would be caused to the **party** or a child if leave were not granted
- the application is for maintenance, and the party applying is on a means-tested pension.

Party or parties—a person or legal entity, such as a corporation, involved in a court case, for example, the applicant or **respondent**.

Respondent—the person named as a party to a case. A respondent may or may not respond to the orders sought by the applicant, in which case they'll be made on the materials that are supplied (i.e. one side won't tell their side of the story).

Couples who were married can consent (that is, agree together) to the matter proceeding out of time without leave being granted (this is just one of the ways in which the law doesn't actually give equal rights to de facto couples).

It is surprising how fast the time goes, and it is very stressful (and expensive) to have to suddenly file an application urgently. Keep the time limits in mind.

Your own bank account and your important documents

If it's safe for you to do so, you should open your own bank account, before or as soon as possible after separation, even if you're still living under the same roof as your ex. Any bank or financial institution will be able to help you with this.

You should arrange for your wages and any other payments (such as Medicare, Centrelink or parenting payments) to be made into your own bank account, in order to protect yourself from your ex helping themselves to your post-separation cash. You should also redirect any direct debits (such as your phone and utilities, for example) to your new bank account so you don't get cut off without realising the bills aren't being paid.

If you receive any family benefits, Centrelink payments or child care rebates, you must also by law inform Centrelink within fourteen days of any changes in your personal circumstances (such as your relationship status and estimated income, and your address if that's changed), which you can do when you're updating your bank account details with them.

You will need a variety of documents to prove your identity in order to open a new bank account. You'll need certified copies or the originals of your important identity documents. More information on which documents you'll need can be found at www.moneysmart.gov.au/managing-your-money/banking/switching-bank-accounts.

On the topic of your important documents, you should try to make copies or take the originals of any of your own documents that you might not have access to post-separation. These include:

- birth certificates (for you and your children)
- marriage certificates
- change of name certificates
- passports (for you and your children)
- immigration certificates
- superannuation statements
- debtors notices
- Medicare cards
- driver's licence
- tax returns
- chequebook (does anyone still have chequebooks?)
- payslips (although most are now electronically available online).

If you can't safely access these documents once you've separated, don't panic. You can access copies of most, if not all, from various government bodies and your bank or financial institutions.

It's also worth noting that a major source of conflict between parents post-separation is who gets to keep the children's passports and birth certificates. Sometimes this can be dealt with in the parenting orders or the parenting plan (and more on this in Chapter 6) but oftentimes they end up staying with the parent who took them in the first place.

What happens in the first few days? And who moves out?

It's a very good idea if one of you can move out as soon as you've decided the marriage is over. If you're the one doing the leaving, try to have a plan about where you'll go once you've had the conversation. Make the plan before you have the talk. Don't leave any doors slightly ajar when you're relaying your decision to your very-soon-to-be-former spouse—if you're really sure, say that. Say, 'I want a divorce, and I'm leaving'. (Or you want a divorce and you want them to leave, which can get a bit trickier—we'll come to this later on.)

It's important to know that the only way to communicate a decision like this is to actually say the words. Don't vacillate, don't pussyfoot around, don't hope they'll take the hint and just somehow disappear.

Use the words, then tell your now-ex that you're staying with your mother, or best mate, or in a hotel, until you've sorted out where everyone is going to live. Living together after the decision has been made to divorce is fraught with danger—legally and personally. Tempers are high, nerves are frayed. If you can start living under separate roofs from the time you've decided the marriage is over, that's a really good start. We'll talk later about how to handle things if you absolutely have to stay cohabitating.

If you've got a piece on the side, admit it like the adult you should be. Don't keep one foot in the door, and really, don't lie. Don't gaslight,[9] and don't give false hope. It's mean and if you've got kids

9 Gaslighting is where you insist that black is white and you don't have a new piece on the side even though you totally do. Be honest.

it will make having any kind of co-parenting relationship so much harder later on.

If your former spouse tells you they're in love with someone else, that's awful, that's horrible, that's a total breach of your trust and your sense of self, and we know how terrible you're feeling. But you will get through this, we absolutely promise. Being told the truth is much better than being trickle-truthed,[10] and makes it much easier for you, in time, to move past this betrayal.

Aside from who lives where, the most important thing during these first few days is to protect yourself emotionally, regardless of whether you're the leaver or the leavee. Your only job for these few days is to get through them.

The dangers of messaging your ex

Both legally and personally, it's very important that you don't send angry, hate-filled text messages to your ex. Or at the very least, try to limit yourself to one a day. You will fail at this, but every time you send a text, think to yourself, 'How will I feel when this goes into an **affidavit** in the Family or Federal Circuit Court—or in an application for a protection order?' Getting it off your chest is not worth it, and it's also potentially evidence that will be used against you.

> **Affidavit**—a written legal statement by a party or witness. An affidavit is a legal version of 'he said, she said'. It's how you present the facts of your case to the court. You must have an affidavit signed before an authorised person (such as a lawyer or Justice of the Peace), and you must swear or attest to the truth of the contents of the affidavit when you speak in court about what you've said in your affidavit. It is an offence to lie in an affidavit. Learning to spell affidavit (and subpoena) takes up almost an entire semester of law school. It's pronounced 'affa-day-vit'.

10 Whereby you find out slowly and over time that actually, you weren't crazy and your partner was cheating on you even though you literally asked them *right* to their face if they were having an affair.

Ask yourself, 'Is this text or email necessary? Is it kind? Is it helpful?' And if the answer is 'None of the above', write it out and send it to your sister, or your best friend, or yourself. Think about the text for a minimum of ten minutes. Set the timer on your phone and then reconsider. Think about what you're really trying to achieve and whether your vicious screed (although totally warranted, no doubt!) gets you there. It can be really embarrassing when your text messages are read out in court, especially if you've taken the opportunity to tell your ex exactly what you've secretly always thought about his mother.

You should also know that your children may read your text messages on the sly, especially if they're older. If you have an iMessage account, then be aware of whether it syncs to your home computer or iPad, especially if your children have access to those devices. Kids are often hypervigilant when their parents are divorcing, and you probably don't want them to read all the lurid details through your texts.

Also, don't throw all of your ex's clothes on the lawn and set them on fire. For one, it's really bad for the grass and if they've left, that grass is now your problem and your problem alone. Secondly, it makes you look like a psycho and they can then say to all your friends and family things like 'You see? *Crazy*. This is why we can't be married any longer.' And you will feel foolish and your best friend will say things like 'Maybe it's time you saw a counsellor?' Not to mention the photographs of the smouldering remains of your ex's wardrobe smoking on the lawn look *really* bad when annexed to your ex's affidavit or an application for a protection order, and it will be something that the children will always remember.

If your ex has had an affair, avoid like the plague the mad 'how to win your spouse back' websites, which counsel things like telling your ex's entire workplace exactly what a nasty cheater your ex is (on infidelity websites, which specialise in parting you from your money, this is called 'affair exposure'). Again, this doesn't work. And anyway, why would you want to be married to someone who cheated on you?

Furthermore, if you have children with the other person, you really do not want them losing their job. You want them paying child support, or otherwise contributing to the financial cost of raising the children.

Try to remember that the only person who looks like a deranged lunatic when you do things like cutting up your ex's clothes is you, and they can get an AVO/DVO[11] against you, which is really bad, expensive to defend, can impact upon your parenting arrangements and can have a serious impact on your employment if you carry a weapon for work. The police may also charge you with malicious damage and this, again, is very bad and expensive to defend.

Don't go to work the day after your marriage ends, unless you really want to—either because you're the type of person who buries their feelings under work, or because you're a neurosurgeon and you're the only one who can separate conjoined twins that day. Otherwise, make a note of the date (you'll need to know the exact date later on for the divorce papers, because you're a sane and organised person and you're on top of things, plus you really don't want to have to ask your ex what the date of your split was) and take the day off work if you can.

Call your mother, call your best mate, and don't panic about the future. You've got plenty of time for the realities, and with this book, you'll have an excellent understanding of the process from here on in.

What about the kids?

You don't need to tell the kids anything today. Take some time to think about how you'd like the news to be shared with them. Think about the unique needs of your kids, and your relationship with them. Think about your ex's relationship with them. A lot of it

11 Domestic and family violence orders are governed by state Acts and are called different things in different states, and although a lot of work has been done to make the laws uniform throughout the country, there are important differences, not least the name of the orders made. The orders tell the person receiving them (known as the defendant or respondent) to not commit domestic violence against the protected person (the aggrieved person or person in need of protection). The orders can also include other conditions such as to stay 100 metres away from the aggrieved or not go to their house. Breaching the orders can result in criminal charges.

will depend on their ages—under twos really don't need to be told anything except 'Daddy (or Mummy) is living in their new house now and you can visit him on Tuesday'. But they don't have to be told today, necessarily (see Chapter 3 for more on this).

It's going to be a hard conversation, and in our experience, it's generally best to take some time to try to get on top of your own emotions before you have it. Having said that, if you cry and gnash your teeth and rent at your clothes and get McDonald's for dinner and announce over Quarter Pounders that Mummy or Daddy have buggered off and are living somewhere else now, the rotten scoundrel, that's totally fine too—you're human. You're going to have human responses.

Cut yourself some slack, especially if you're dealing with a bombshell. You're not Gwyneth Paltrow or Chris Martin—you're not consciously uncoupling, you're getting D-I-V-O-R-C-E-D *and it's horrible.*

Part of cutting yourself some slack is to start the process of learning that your former spouse is not your soft place to fall anymore—if in fact they ever were. Chances are, you'll miss the idea of them far more than the reality of living with them. So don't call them, don't text them, don't beg, don't engage at all for these first few days.

And *don't* agree to *anything* in relation to property division or child access arrangements. You have time for all of that, but that time is not today, or even next week. Definitely don't agree to anything until you have spoken to a lawyer.

'Experts' say (or we read somewhere in *Psychology Today*, which actually does totally count, thank you very much) that it takes slightly less than half the length of a relationship to get over the end of that relationship, which will initially seem utterly horrifying but seems roughly to be true.

Most of all, be kind to yourself.

And step away from your phone.

2

The first week

So now it's a week later. You've gotten through the first seven days, and it's probably time you thought about calling a family lawyer. First up, though, here are a few facts about how the **jurisdiction** of family law is divvied up in Australia. It's a bit boring and technical, so bear with us.

> **Jurisdiction**—the legal authority that a judge or a court has to act or make decisions in a given situation or case.

The jurisdiction of the family law courts

Family law in Australia is a federal jurisdiction. The *Family Law Act 1975* (Cth) (this means Commonwealth) is the main law that applies. The Family Law Act is an Act of the Australian Parliament, not state parliaments. Family law in Australia is therefore pretty much 'uniform' across the country.

With the exception of Western Australia, which has its own family court, there are two family law courts in Australia—the Federal Circuit Court, which deals with garden-variety separations and divorces, and the Family Court of Australia, which deals with more complicated issues and cases. If you get divorced in Western

Australia, just to be even more painful about it, then the federal Act applies, but if you're in a de facto relationship then the state Act applies.

Since 2009, in most of Australia (except, again, annoyingly Western Australia), property settlements between de facto partners are dealt with under the Act and in the Federal Circuit Court and Family Court of Australia.

Parenting matters between de facto couples have been dealt with under the Act and in the family law courts since the late 1980s and early 1990s, except in, where else, but Western Australia.

Local and magistrates courts have some jurisdiction as well and sometimes consent orders (which we'll talk about in a lot of detail later on) can be made through them, to keep things interesting, we guess.

How to choose a lawyer

Firstly, if you're feeling really terrible, it's a good idea to get both a psychologist and a lawyer. Psychologists, who charge about $180 an hour,[12] are much cheaper than lawyers, who charge about $300 to more than $600. Your lawyer is not your counsellor, and every single time you send him or her 'just a quick email' or make 'just a quick call' to check on something, that's going to go on your bill.

Except for some limited circumstances involving family violence, child abuse or abduction, it is usually compulsory to have family dispute resolution (mediation) before going to court regarding parenting matters.

Family violence and **abuse** are defined in the Family Law Act as:

> **Abuse**—in relation to a child, means:
>
> - an assault, including a sexual assault, of the child
> - a person (the first person) involving the child in a sexual activity with the first person or another person in which the child is used, directly or indirectly, as a sexual object

12 Many workplaces provide confidential psychologist services at no cost through Employee Assistance Programs. You can also access discounted counselling through Medicare, which we discuss further in Chapter 3.

by the first person or the other person, and where there is unequal power in the relationship between the child and the first person

- causing the child to suffer serious psychological harm, including (but not limited to) when that harm is caused by the child being subjected to, or exposed to, family violence

or

- serious neglect of the child.[13]

Family violence—violent, threatening or other behaviour by a person that coerces or controls a member of the person's family (the family member), or causes the family member to be fearful. Examples of behaviour that may constitute family violence include (but are not limited to):

- an assault
- a sexual assault or other sexually abusive behaviour
- stalking
- repeated derogatory taunts
- intentionally damaging or destroying property
- intentionally causing death or injury to an animal
- unreasonably denying the family member the financial autonomy that they would otherwise have had
- unreasonably withholding financial support needed to meet the reasonable living expenses of the family member, or their child, at a time when the family member is entirely or predominantly dependent on the person for financial support
- preventing the family member from making or keeping connections with their family, friends or culture
- unlawfully depriving the family member, or any member of the family member's family, of their liberty.[14]

It is a good idea to get some legal advice before you go to mediation so that you have the best possible chance of success, and to give

13 Section 4 *Family Law Act 1975*.
14 Section 4AB *Family Law Act 1975*.

you the best possible chance of an outcome that you can live with. Your lawyer will go through options, the mediation process, the documents that you will need and the law relevant to your matter, so you are prepared and can negotiate from a position of knowledge and strength. We'll talk much (much) more about this in Chapter 6.

Choosing a lawyer can be really tough, and it's not something people do every day. You may not know where to even start. There's also a difference between the lawyers you can access through Legal Aid, through a private law firm, or through a community or women's legal service. We'll go through the differences below.

Legal Aid

Legal Aid provides free, or discounted, legal advice and representation in family law matters, which generally covers 'issues arising from family breakdown (especially matters involving children), domestic and family violence, and child support'.[15] Legal Aid is a state-based service, so it varies a bit from state to state.

Legal Aid also provides duty lawyers at some courts, including most major registries of the Federal Circuit Court and the Family Court. Duty lawyers generally give advice only (that is, they don't represent you in court or write nasty letters on your behalf to your ex). In some states Legal Aid does not provide legal representation in property matters, which means the process of dividing your assets or your debts. In other states Legal Aid will provide funding for property matters; it is best to contact Legal Aid in your state to see if you can obtain assistance from them.

Some private firms are also Legal Aid preferred suppliers and can represent you under a grant of aid (this means they are paid by Legal Aid, but are lawyers who work in a private law firm).

The Legal Aid form can be a bit daunting and you can be rejected for aid if you get it wrong. If you do get stuck filling out the form, a community legal service lawyer or a Legal Aid lawyer (or even a private lawyer) can help you even if you haven't yet been granted Legal Aid.

---

15 www.legalaid.nsw.gov.au.

Legal Aid is means tested, and as it is funded by the state and territory governments, there's no one figure we can give you to help you work out if you'll be eligible. Generally speaking, if you rely on Centrelink benefits as your sole source of income, and don't have a lot of equity in your home or don't own a home, you'll most likely be eligible.

If you earn wages, or have other financial help, then you can earn up to a certain amount each week before you have to contribute to the cost of the Legal Aid lawyer. In Queensland, as at August 2017, you can earn up to $370 a week as a single person without having to pay a co-payment fee, but the formula changes depending on how much you earn over that amount and how many children you have, and also depends on what assets you own, including your home and your car.

In Resources, we've provided the addresses for each of the Legal Aid websites across the states and territories.

What if I'm not eligible for a grant of Legal Aid?

If you're not eligible for a grant of Legal Aid, you can find advice and limited representation through a community legal centre, or you will have to find a private lawyer. You can also be self-represented, which we'll discuss below.

Self-representing

Lawyers are really expensive. Even comfortably well-off people may find that with their family income literally halving overnight, the cost of lawyers is prohibitive. We understand that, which is partly why we wrote this book. Access to justice shouldn't be just the preserve of the very wealthy. There is no reason why you can't run many aspects of your matter yourself, and seek advice when you need it.

There's also heaps of information available online, although it's important to sort the wheat from the chaff, because some of the sites we've seen give misleading or out-of-date information you don't want to rely on. The websites of the family law courts (Family Court of Australia,[16] Federal Circuit Court[17] and Family Court of Western

16 www.familycourt.gov.au/wps/wcm/connect/fcoaweb/home.

17 www.federalcircuitcourt.gov.au/wps/wcm/connect/fccweb/home.

Australia[18]) have huge amounts of helpful, plain English resources available and should be the first place you look if you need a quick answer to a question.

Where you will find it tricky is when you need to speak up in court or provide cases to back up your position (otherwise known as **precedents**).

> **Precedent**—a decision made by a judicial officer, which may serve as an example for other cases or orders, unless the judge decides the facts of the case are too different.

Understanding how the courts have decided these cases (**case law**), and the way they approached them, is a key lawyer skill, and it's why lawyers are expensive—they have to spend about 40 per cent of their waking hours reading case law to keep on top of all the latest developments.

> **Case law**—law that has been made by a judge or judges, that is binding, and becomes precedent (see: **Precedent**). (See also: unhelpful.)

Private lawyers

A private lawyer is a lawyer that you pay for by yourself. The best way to choose a private lawyer is through word of mouth, although most people start out by googling local family lawyers. If you feel comfortable doing so, ask around for details of lawyers who people you know have used and been happy with. Always remember, though, you have to have confidence in your lawyer, and different lawyers will suit different people.

Many lawyers will offer free or reduced rates for first consultations or free phone consultations, and if you don't gel with the lawyer in that meeting, you don't have to use them. Some people may prefer a woman, some a man. It really is up to you.

18 www.familycourt.wa.gov.au.

Community/women's legal services

Community legal services, women's legal services and the Aboriginal Legal Service are exceptional organisations that provide (generally) free legal advice, help with applying for Legal Aid, some assistance with drafting documents (although this may be limited), limited representation in court, and referrals.

Lawyers from these services won't represent you in court as a general rule, nor will they handle your 'matter' for you from start to finish. Their services are more designed to give you general advice and to help you access other services through referrals.

Some community legal services (such as Caxton Legal Centre in Brisbane) have duty lawyers available at courts.

Referrals can be to Legal Aid or to a private lawyer. Referrals can also be to organisations like Relationships Australia or a Family Relationship Centre, which can provide **family dispute resolution** (mediation), counselling and other support. You can find a community legal service near you at: www.naclc.org.au/.

> **Family dispute resolution**—(or FDR) a process where a family dispute resolution practitioner assists people to try to resolve some or all of their disputes with each other following separation and/or divorce. (Most people just call this mediation but the government can't resist a good three-letter acronym.)

Conflict check

A conflict check is something lawyers have to do before they can represent you. For example, it's possible that another lawyer in your lawyer's firm has already taken on your ex as a client. That means they can't now work for you. This can happen often in small towns, where there may not be many family lawyers. It also applies to Legal Aid—if they are representing your ex, they may not be able to represent you. This can be very upsetting, especially if money is tight, and your ex has nabbed the 'best' lawyer in town. But as hard as it is, the same firm or organisation can't represent the same two parties in a case—it's an unacceptable conflict and not allowed by law.

In circumstances where the conflict check doesn't check out, the firm that can't act for you may refer you to another lawyer.

The psychology of divorce, or why do I feel so bad about my separation?

All this is really hard. As we've discussed, for many, many people separation and divorce is the second most horrible thing they can go through. And there's a reason for that—it's called the human condition. Psychology can, and does, explain why we feel so awful when we're facing a break-up—and it basically comes down to the different stages of grief, and attachment theory.

Stages of grief

So let's talk about the stages of grief. We're going to come back to this quite a bit, because it's critically important that you understand how grief (which is what you experience at the end of a relationship) works and how each individual stage works.

One thing we found really important is accepting that people grieve differently, and at different rates. If you made the decision to end the marriage, you've done a fair bit of your grieving already, and you've moved through the various stages. But if you're totally blindsided, you have to start at stage one.

If you've left your partner after a long period of reflection and thought, you might be at stage five, and it might seem really tedious that your soon-to-be-ex is wallowing (in your mind) in stage one. Be kind, and patient. Grief is a process, and it takes time.

Often the person leaving the relationship has been through a long grieving process themselves and may not have been emotionally or physically available to the other party or children. The other party may be furious that not only have they put up with what they see as bad behaviour from their partner, but now, to top it all off, their partner is leaving. The fury may be much worse if there is a third party involved, and this can drive some pretty intense behaviour.

If you are the new partner, please accept that there is nothing useful that you can say or do with respect to the partner left behind. If this new relationship is to be long term and there are kids, you're going to have to be involved with the parenting to some degree in the future and what you do now is going to set the tone for your relationship with your new partner's ex for a long time to come. If you love and support your partner, then the best thing you can do is be supportive of their relationship with the other parent of their children. Only sociopaths would try to ruin that critically important relationship out of some misplaced sense of jealousy.

Accepting that your new partner's ex is going through the absolute worst time possible is going to help here (but telling them that is not going to help at all), as is accepting that they are going through their stages of grief and keeping out of the way for now.

Elisabeth Kübler-Ross, the brilliant pioneer of hospice care, defined the stages of grief as follows (our commentary in brackets):

Denial
('This is not happening to me. She's just going through a midlife crisis. We will work things out.')

Anger and resentment
('How can he do this to me? I hate him! I wish he was dead! He owes me for everything I have done for him!')

Bargaining
('Stay, and I'll accept that you're secretly gay. Stay, and we'll have an open marriage. Stay, and I'll be a better spouse. Stay, and I'll transmorph myself into a Stepford Wife even more than I already have.')

Depression
('I am so sad I feel like I will never get over this. I will die old and alone and my cats (note: must get cats) will eat my face off.')

Acceptance
('I can, and I am, getting through this. I know my own value. I will be happy again.')

Once you understand that you're grieving the end of a relationship (even if you ended it and it was truly awful anyway), it's easier to see the process as just that—a process, which you have to go through.

There are no shortcuts, no workarounds—you have to do the hard emotional work of grief, unless, of course, you're particularly adept at stuffing down your emotions only to have them come out at inappropriate times, or you find a rebound relationship to distract you (these are all fine choices, but possibly not the healthiest long term).

If you're having a really hard time, talking to a therapist can help label your emotions and talk them through in a safe, neutral place.

Attachment theory

Having a basic understanding of attachment theory can also help you understand why your emotions are all over the place, or why you're *so* upset even if the divorce was all your idea.

Attachment theory,[19] in our opinion, explains almost everything there is to know about human behaviour, and it's something a psychologist can really help you understand better.

There's a simple test for working out who your primary attachment bond is with, and it's this:

> You are sitting at your desk, and the phone rings. It's your boss, and you've gotten the big promotion!
>
> Or, you are sitting at your desk, and the phone rings. It's your boss; your position has been abolished, and you're being made redundant.
>
> Who do you call in both instances?

Most people in a relationship, no matter how toxic, will ring their partner when the news is good and when the news is bad. During a divorce, one of the hardest things many people face is the loss of their primary attachment partner. *Attachment* isn't the same as

19 J Bowlby, 'The influence of early environment in the development of neurosis and neurotic character', *International Journal of Pyschoanalysis*, 1, 1940.

intimacy, and it's possible to be very strongly attached to someone while at the same time not being particularly close to them at all.

The overwhelming sense of loss and fear that goes along with thinking about a break-up is what keeps many people in a toxic relationship far longer than they should be. It's what triggers rebound relationships, and exit affairs—the human need to not be all alone in this world. A primary attachment is 'a lasting psychological connectedness between two human beings'[20] and it's not something we *desire*, it's something we *need*.

Primary attachment, and the ability to form a strong and stable emotional bond, is formed from birth, generally with your mother. As we mature, our primary attachment (so long as we've had good modelling of what a secure attachment is) usually transfers relatively seamlessly to our partners. We'll come back to attachment theory when we discuss negotiating your child access arrangements in Chapter 6, because it's super important in that context as well.

When a baby doesn't have a secure primary attachment (such as when their needs are not met by a loving, consistent caregiver), their primary bonding can be disrupted, and they learn to meet their own needs through self-soothing techniques.

This can result in arrested development,[21] and some pretty cruel experiments showed that baby monkeys, when deprived of contact with their mothers, developed bizarre and self-destructive behaviours such as biting their own arms and legs, obsessive self-rocking, and clinging to fabric rag dolls as a mother-substitute. They were also bullied by the other monkeys once they were reintroduced to the group.

The baby monkeys who were isolated for a year never recovered and never learnt to form a primary attachment with any other monkey. Other experiments on poor baby monkeys show that when deprived of their mothers, the monkeys grew up to have difficulty finding mates and made poor parents themselves.

The point of all this is not just to show how awful psychological experiments in the 1960s were, but to show that primary attachment

20 ibid.
21 Not the band, or the TV show (both great, though).

theory explains a lot when it comes to the often overwhelming grief people feel when faced with divorce. One woman we know explained it as 'always feeling homesick, even when I was at home with my children'.

This is a horrible way to feel, and it's why it's pretty hard to get over someone if you're talking to them every day and still relying on them for emotional support (this is regardless of who left who). Breaking your primary attachment to your soon-to-be-ex-spouse is a critical step in healing.

It's an especially hard thing for the spouse who ultimately leaves the marital home, and who is faced with the reality of life apart from their kids, their neighbourhood, and everything that anchors them to their personal life.

The good news is that a period of no contact can help weaken a primary attachment, which is crucial if you are to get over your ex in a romantic sense and form a new, healthy relationship with them post-separation. No contact means no contact of any type as far as possible, particularly if there is abuse, a history of being on again/off again, emotional game-playing, or any kind of general nastiness.

But it is unquestionably hard to do, because you're trying to break your primary attachment. You have to unfriend them on Facebook, not stalk their Instagram, drop them from LinkedIn. Block their phone number so they can't call you or message you, after letting them know that in an emergency they can call your mum or dad or best friend, who will get a message to you. Communicate only via email, and only about things like arrangements for the children, which has the added bonus of being a written record of your communications in case you need it later.

If the split is very nasty, and you're engaging in unhealthy shouting matches over the phone and finding that you're constantly relitigating every aspect of your relationship and split, don't engage with your ex at all. That's what your lawyer is for. Try to be the Grey Rock. [22]

22 Being the Grey Rock is a common technique for reducing conflict by refusing to engage. Picture yourself as a big, grey rock in an ocean, being battered by waves from all sides. But you don't care about the waves, because you're a grey rock—nothing can move you.

Case study—Jessica and Jason

Jessica and Jason had been married for twelve years, although they'd been together for over twenty, since they were teenagers. They had three children, Sophia, Natalia and Imogen, aged ten, eight and six.

It was an incredibly toxic relationship. Both Jessica and Jason had frequently cheated and Jason had had a long-term affair, which he found very hard to break off. They talked about nothing except the children and had been sleeping in separate rooms for three years. They were both completely miserable, fought constantly, and there had been several extremely frightening incidents of domestic violence, which seemed to be escalating. The children had witnessed all of these incidents.

Over the past three years, both Jessica and Jason repeatedly tried to end the relationship. At the same time, neither could seem to do it. One or the other would always come back home, almost straight away, and they would both sweep the whole thing under the carpet—until the next blow-up.

Eventually, after a particularly nasty physical fight that was witnessed by their neighbours, they sought counselling, and they learnt that they had a codependent relationship that was based on their mutual fear of being poor and alone with the children.

Jessica realised that the relationship was damaging both her self-esteem and sense of self-worth, and was a toxic environment in which to raise her children. She moved into a rented house with the children, engaged a lawyer and commenced legal proceedings (including a plan for the children that meant all changeovers occurred at school),[23] and didn't

23 'Changeovers' are where your child or children go from your care to their other parent's care or back again. For example, if your children are dropped at your front door by your ex, that's a changeover. If you drop the children to school at 9 a.m. and he picks them up at 3.10 p.m., that's a changeover.

communicate directly with Jason for six months. The separation stuck, and Jessica felt free for the first time in her adult life.

Just because you have a very strong attachment to someone doesn't mean that the attachment is healthy. A good psychologist can help you unpack why you're so miserable, even if intellectually you know that divorce is the best thing for you, and for your children, if you have them.

Breaking an unhealthy attachment can often be the first step in rebuilding your better, happier, post-divorce life, and finding joy again.

WORKSHEET 1
WHO WILL BE MY SUPPORT PEOPLE?

You will need people around you to support you through this process. Some will be people you pay, others will be your close friends and family.

Don't be worried about asking for help—all this really means is a quick text (for some) to ask if you can rely on them occasionally, or a meeting (with the school, for example) to let them know what's going on and how you might need help (accessing the school counsellor, giving your kids extra support in class, helping with access to after-school care programs, etc.).

People will want to help you. Lots and lots of people ask other people for help every day—why shouldn't you?

In the worksheet below, you can plan who your support people will be, and how you will utilise them.

This list could include people such as:

- your lawyer
- good friends
- neighbours
- your boss
- your colleagues
- former colleagues
- your school-mum or school-dad friends
- your mum
- your dad
- brothers and sisters
- extended family
- your church and church leaders, if you're religious
- your children's friends
- your children's day care educators or school teachers, or after-school carers
- your general practitioner
- your psychologist
- your local domestic violence support liaison
- the local police, if you are dealing with domestic violence.

MY SUPPORT PEOPLE WORKSHEET

Support person	Support capacity (i.e. legal, emotional, child care)	How they can help	Date you discussed with them your need for help
Example: Jane Eyre, Jane Eyre and Associates	Lawyer	With my legal requirements	Appointment made 1 March 2017

3

Telling your children and extended family

You've talked to your lawyer. Hey—you've got a lawyer! Well done. You've even got your first conference scheduled (more on what to do here in Chapter 5). Your lawyer seems nice, but more importantly they seem competent and you're clear that they're not your counsellor, they're someone you're paying $600 an hour to sort this situation out for you.

> **Conference**—a meeting between lawyers and / or barristers and their clients. Most people would call this a meeting, but lawyers aren't most people.

Okay. Now it's time to tell the kids, if you've got them, that Mummy or Daddy hasn't just been travelling a lot for work lately or that you're taking some time out to think things through, but that you're getting divorced (and if you don't have kids, feel free to skip ahead to the end of this chapter where we talk about 'how to tell your ninety-year-old grandma you're getting divorced'—pro tip: make your mother do it).

This is a terrible conversation for you, and for your kids, no matter how old they are (unless they're literally pre-verbal). You might still be snot-crying but hopefully you've taken a few days, possibly even a week, to gather your thoughts and now you're as ready as you can be.

It's easy to make the stupid mistake of doing the big okay-kids-sit-down-we-all-need-to-talk thing when really, it's as plain as the noses on all of your faces that something's up.

The most important things to consider are:

- the ages of your kids
- how your ex wants to tell them
- and how *you* want to tell them.

Firstly, going to divorce counselling (cheaper than a lawyer!) can be a good idea. If you're feeling up to it and you don't want to scratch your ex's stupid face clean off (and if you do want to, that's cool—you're still in Anger), you can give it a go.

Divorce counselling is where you talk to a third-party counsellor about how you're going to handle the emotional, and practical, work of your divorce together with your former spouse. It can work if you're reasonably amicable and have mutually decided on a divorce, but need a little help with the logistics. We've heard it used well when after a long period of marriage counselling, both parties decide to call it quits and then use the same counsellor to help them reach consensus on key points around the children and the assets.

Otherwise, you'll probably fall into camp B, which is the rest of us. In this camp, we negotiate delivering the most devastating news our children will (hopefully!) ever hear over nasty texts and through hissed conversations. Someone will take the moral high ground and even though the view is great, it's not helpful. Climb on down, and we'll chat about what is.

If you've already told your kids that their other parent has left or is leaving, and you maybe didn't do it the way a child psychology textbook might tell you to, don't beat yourself up. Being a super-parent is almost impossible even when all your needs are being met, you're in the happiest relationship in the world, and you're surrounded by a village of adoring relatives. It's (in our experience, anyway) almost impossible to be the parent you would best like to be when you're heartbroken and angry. Anger is a natural stage of grief and you're a human being. It's okay.

(As an aside, isn't it funny how your ex-spouse almost immediately shifts from being 'Daddy' or 'Mummy' to 'your father' or 'your mother' when you're talking to your kids about their other parent?)

But of course, if you can, it's better to try to do this sort of thing the 'right' way. So if you haven't already told your kids that their no-good, deadbeat loser of a parent has effed off, to save you the effort of googling 'ways to tell kids about divorce', we've helpfully curated the top tips, and broken them down into age groups. These are meant to be read cumulatively, so read each stage if you can, because each stage builds on the previous stage—and you don't want to miss out on our rantings, after all.

Don't divide and conquer

It was Abraham Lincoln who said 'a house divided against itself cannot stand'. And he was onto something there. If, like lots of us, you decided that a super-fun way to spend your twenties and thirties was to have kids very well spaced out (which means that you literally have a preschooler at home for fourteen continuous years), you're going to have kids at different stages of childhood.

However, it's very important (according to psychologist Kevin D Arnold PhD) to tell all your kids together, and to tell them the same thing, no matter how old they are.[24] The message can be tailored to each child, sure, but the bottom line is—don't make your older kids your secret-keeper. After all, look at how that worked out for the Potters.[25] Don't make one kid responsible for keeping the secret from his or her brothers or sisters, because they probably won't be able to, which will make them feel guilty, and they'll resent you for it down the track.

---

24 Kevin D. Arnold PhD, 'Mom and dad have something to tell you', *Pyschology Today*, 2011, https://www.psychologytoday.com/blog/the-older-dad/201105/mom-and-dad-have-something-tell-you-six-tips-talking-kids-about-divorce.

25 This is a Harry Potter reference—if you haven't read the books yet, think about reading them to your kids, or listening to the audiobooks together! It's a lovely story of redemption and hope and a great family tradition to start post-separation.

Case study—Leonie and Tara

Leonie and Tara had been together for twelve years. They had two children, Kit (aged ten) and Mira (aged six). Both Leonie and Tara had joint parental responsibility for Kit and Mira, although Leonie was the biological mother of Kit, and Tara was the biological mother of Mira.

Leonie decided that she would tell Kit that she and Tara were splitting up one night while Tara was at work and while Mira was in bed. She didn't tell Mira. Kit was very confused, and was anxious that she had been asked to keep a secret from her little sister. The next day she asked Tara if she was still going to be her mother, and if she would ever see Mira again.

Unbeknown to anyone, Mira was hiding on the stairs and heard the whole thing, which is how she learnt that her mothers were separating.

Tara, furious, rang Leonie at work and tore strips off her. It wasn't a great conversation for anyone and Leonie felt even more awful than she already did.

Together or apart?

The accepted wisdom is that you should sit down with your ex-spouse and your kids and tell the kids all together 'as a family'. Which is all well and good if there are no restraining orders, no violence, no white-hot anger and no Other Woman or Other Man lurking in the background. Don't put yourself in danger, emotionally or physically, in order 'to do the right thing'. There's no law that says you have to tell the kids together. If your ex gets mad at you for telling the kids, then too bad, so sad. You haven't broken any law.

If you're amicable, then of course, knock yourselves out, but if the idea of sitting in a room with your ex while they lecture the children about why they're leaving makes you want to throw up, then don't put yourself through it. Nobody can or should make you, and it doesn't make you a good or bad parent either way.

Case study—Alice and Brad

After fifteen years together, Alice discovered that Brad had been having an affair. Brad, being a jerk, said to Alice, 'It's not really cheating if we're not actually legally married'. They had six children, all of whom had unpronounceable names.

Brad got himself an apartment but Alice suspected (and she was right) that this was mere window-dressing, and that Brad had in fact moved in with his affair partner, Jane.

Brad, after months of neglecting his family in order to woo Jane, now decided that he was Super Dad and pressured Alice to 'tell the kids together' that the marriage was definitely over and they were getting divorced so that they knew 'we would always be a family'. He argued that this was the 'adult and mature way of handling things'. He also mentioned that in his opinion Alice was 'being a bit childish'.

Alice told Brad he could get stuffed and told the six kids by herself as they were finishing up dinner one night.

Setting the scene

Brad and Alice's story brings us to another point—where should you tell the children? One website says 'don't tell the kids in the car!' Another says 'telling your kids in the car while on the way somewhere can provide an easy, calm and relaxed opportunity to break the news'.

So the answer here seems to be—there's no right way. It's horrible news. They'll remember this moment forever. They're your kids, and you know them best. Short of filming it in public and putting it on Facebook (don't do this), you'll know the best setting. We'd probably suggest one Saturday afternoon, in your own home, so your kids have a bit of time to digest the news and ask questions before a new week starts. But that's just us, and our families, and might seem like a terrible idea to you. Do it where you feel most comfortable.

Ages 0–2

People might tell you that it's 'easiest' to get divorced when your kids are still barely sentient. This is untrue. Getting divorced when your kids are two is just as sucky as getting divorced when your kids are twenty-two. Two-year-olds are not toilet-trained, and twenty-two-year-olds have *opinions*.

When you're getting divorced and your kids are under two, the message will be very simple, by virtue of the fact that your child hasn't fully mastered the English language (or indeed any language). You can say something like 'Mummy and Daddy are going to live in/are living in different houses'.

You could also read them a storybook, such as *Two Homes* by Claire Masurel or *Dinosaurs Divorce* by Laurene Krasny Brown and Marc Brown, or our favourite, *When Mama Comes Home Tonight* by Eileen Spinelli, which is a gorgeous story about a single mum coming home from work to her baby. It's not really about divorce, but about different families, and how a mum and a baby are absolutely a family.[26]

Most of all, offer your baby lots of cuddles and reassurance, tell them that you love them, and tell them who will look after them, and try to keep to your routine. There's not a lot you can say at this age that will be understood, so for this age group, you keeping your act together as best you possibly can (or asking someone, like your mum, to help you for a little while), is probably the most important thing.

Ages 2–4

Beautiful little souls are a bit more on the ball at this age. The storybook suggestions for the 0–2 age group will also work well, and can help bring about a conversation a little more naturally.

Here, it's important that your child knows who is going to be looking after them, and how often they'll be seeing the other parent. We know it's hard, but really, try not to badmouth your former spouse. We read once that badmouthing your ex feels to a child like

26 And so are a dad and a baby!

you're badmouthing them. This can take superhuman strength and is for some of us a day-to-day challenge, especially in the early days.

Tell your kids that Mummy/Daddy is moving out, because Mummy and Daddy want to be friends instead of being married to each other. We personally think the line 'Mummy and Daddy fight too much to live together' is a bit problematic, because siblings often fight like cats and dogs (actually our cats and dogs don't fight at all, they avoid each other like the plague) and then the kids will think, 'Well, Amelia and me fight all the time, and we still have to live together; why can't Mum and Dad?'

So, avoid that line and go with the friends line instead. Yes, it feels a bit 'it's not you it's me' but they're children, they'll fall for bad lines. Then give them the information they need about their daily routines (like 'Mummy will drop you off at daycare and ~~your father~~ Daddy will pick you up'). Children of this age just want to know how it's going to affect them, because they are still self-centric—their world revolves around their needs.

This is an evolutionary survival tool, and it's important that you provide lots of reassurance and simple explanations, and again, keep their routines going as much as you possibly can.

It's also a nice idea to start a new family tradition—in Lucy's family, post-separation, we started a Sunday night dinner tradition with our close friends who live nearby, and it's been a key aspect of our post-divorce social life, and a real source of joy. You might find your toddler becomes a bit clingy post-separation, which is totally normal, and new traditions can help ease the transition a little.

Unless your ex is a real piece of work who's already moved in with the next victim, kids at this age can help their parents find, furnish and decorate their new digs. This can really help your kids feel a sense of ownership of their new home/s, and can actually be a bit of fun. Ask your kids to help, and ask them especially to help pick out stuff for their new room—if funds are tight, check out places like Kmart, where you can pick up funky kids furnishings inexpensively.

Ages 4–7

All the stuff in the previous two age groups applies, but at this stage, you'll need to provide a bit more information and extra reassurances. Leave lots of time for questions, and listen more than you talk.

Your kids will want to know more by way of details—about how their lives will change, who will be looking after them, whether they'll be changing schools or moving homes, and why you're getting a divorce.

At this age, kids are developing lives outside of the home. Their friendship groups are becoming more important, and they are a (little) less self-involved. You'll be able to discuss why you and your ex can't live together anymore in more age-appropriate detail, but the basic line about 'being friends' still seems to be the go, according to the experts, even though kids this age will have picked up on the tension and fighting in the household. Being as honest as you can about the fact that Mummy or Daddy doesn't live at home anymore is important, because kids get anxious when they're not quite sure what's going on.

Or, they might know exactly what's going on, despite your best efforts to only fight at night when you think they're all asleep. They may have overheard specifics of your fights, and you may have to deal directly with specific questions, and once again, age-appropriate honesty is the best policy.

Infidelity

At this juncture we'll pause to talk about infidelity. It's common for kids to pick sides and blame one parent over another for the divorce, especially if they've worked out there's infidelity involved, but try not to revel in this too much if you're holding the moral high ground.

It's important to remember that the law literally doesn't care if there's been infidelity in the relationship. In Australia, as you probably know, we have 'no fault' divorce, where you don't need to give a reason for the end of the relationship, beyond the fact that one or both of you states that it has 'irretrievably broken down'. So, the fact that your ex is a big fat cheater won't affect anything to do with the arrangements for the kids, or the property settlement. This will seem astonishingly unfair but that's the way it is, baby. It would be much worse if we still had the old at fault system where you could only get a divorce if your spouse was clinically insane, or you could prove infidelity, which led to lots of private detectives following people around in the dark and didn't really help anyone move on gracefully.

We know from a mountain of research that the most damaging thing for kids about divorce isn't the divorce, it's the acrimony between separated parents, which obviously can be greatly exacerbated by cheating. As angry as you may be, try to hold in your heart the idea that the best outcome for you and for your kids is if you can minimise conflict.

The first step towards this is to try to actually minimise conflict post-separation, and not just in front of the kids. They hear everything! This is where strict no contact (remember Chapter 2) in the first few weeks or months, except via email and only when necessary, is so important if you're really angry.

There's lots of conflicting information about whether or not you should talk to your kids about infidelity as a reason for your divorce. In some cases, your ex will have moved in with their new 'partner' and so it's pretty clear what's gone down to everyone, kids included. People in the bubble of infidelity justify these sorts of actions to themselves in lots of different ways, such as by thinking crazy things like 'Our love is real and worth hurting people for'[27] and 'Kids are resilient and they'll get over it'.

The nastiest divorces we know of as family lawyers are all ones that featured infidelity—and if you're at all keen on having a functional co-parenting relationship with your ex within this decade, cheating on them is a really good way of making sure that doesn't happen. We know that when a new client turns up and they say, 'My partner is cheating on me', it's going to be a doozy of a divorce.

It's also very hurtful to children. Our society is extremely anti-cheating—you will be stunned how many messages your children will be exposed to that portray cheaters as the scum of the

27 Adapted from Soul Mate Schmoopies, www.soulmateschmoopies.wordpress.com.

earth. As someone who was cheated on, you will feel both vindicated and horrified by the messages your children are receiving about their other parent.

The best advice we could find about telling kids that your marriage has ended because of an affair is to examine your own motivations for doing so.[28] Is it to hurt your ex and inflict damage on them in the eyes of their children? Or is it because the actions of your ex are such that telling the truth is the only thing that will make sense to your children (for instance, if the new partner is on the scene immediately)? When you look at your motivations, try to remove your own emotional responses from your decision, and think about what your children need to know in order for them to understand why their parents are getting divorced.

But overall, we think the truth almost always outs, and constructing an untrue narrative isn't going to stick for long. If your children figure out later on that there was infidelity, and you've kept that a secret, that can erode their trust in you, because really, it's a form of gaslighting, isn't it? Denying what they long suspected?

If you do tell your kids that your marriage ended because of infidelity, keep the story simple. You can just say, 'Mummy and Daddy were not happy being married to each other anymore, and Mummy wanted to ~~be a skank with her boyfriend~~ be John's girlfriend'.

The fact is, when you're recovering from a divorce caused by infidelity, it's very hard to parent according to the textbooks. You're probably going to be really angry, and resentful, and vengeful. Your ex on the other hand has done their grieving and has moved on with unseemly haste, and is happily ensconced in a new relationship.

Probably their household income hasn't halved (most cheaters meet their new partners at work) and probably they're not facing a housing and employment crisis. Meanwhile, you're left with the reality of being a sole parent, of having to rehome yourself, find new employment, new schools, and do a thousand other things to organise and sort out your new life.

---

28 Scott Haltzman, MD, 'Should the children know you've had an affair?', *Psychology Today*, 2013, www.psychologytoday.com/blog/surviving-infidelity/201305/should-the-children-know-youve-had-affair.

You've had a very nasty shock and the person you are most attached to in the whole world is suddenly treating you like this is all somehow your fault (it's not, nothing you did or didn't do can justify being cheated on). It's vitally important that you find good people you can lean on so you can function, and who will listen to you say the same thing over and over again for months on end.

You will find out who your real friends are, and this is a horrible lesson at a time when really, you're not massively in need of another Horrible Life Lesson. But on the other hand, people who you would never have expected to will step up to love and support you.

In addition to leaning on your friends and your family, go to your GP and ask for a mental health plans which can give you access to up to sixteen sessions with a therapist (subject to eligibility criteria) at a much reduced rate.[29]

If your partner has left you with small kids and moved in with their Soul Mate Schmoopie,[30] don't feel under any obligation to meet their new paramour, even if they are going to be spending time with your kids. If you're not up to it, don't do it. There's no legal obligation to do so.

If you're never up to it, don't worry about it. You do not legally have to have any kind of relationship with this Other Person, and nobody can make you. If you choose, they do not need to be a part of your life at all and that's completely fine.

Oftentimes, however, it's the case that eventually everything settles down and even very nasty divorces involving infidelity can translate into good co-parenting relationships where you eventually remember that you quite like your former spouse. In fact, at one point you liked them enough to have children with them. You may even find that the Other Person is, despite their pretty reprehensible behaviour, a halfway decent character who can help when you and your ex are both stuck in traffic and the kids have to be picked up from afterschool care.

---

29 The Better Access to Psychiatrists, Psychologists and General Practitioners through the Medicare Benefits Schedule (Better Access) initiative.

30 Google Soul Mate Schmoopies! It's hilarious.

To get to this point takes time and kindness. If you've been the cheater, then you have an obligation to be kind to your ex without giving false hope. You should also go to your GP to get a referral to a psychologist to help you find a way to make the best of the mess you've made. And you must remember that your ex-spouse needs time to accept the new reality of their life—you've done all your grieving about the end of the relationship, and they are just starting, plus you've got someone to help mop up your pain, and they (probably) don't.

You should also be aware that there will be a number of people in your life who either know, or strongly suspect, you are cheating, and they may include your partner and children.

Case study—Martin and Heather

Martin and Heather were both forty-seven, and had been married for seventeen years when Martin received a text one morning while he was in the shower. Heather, being helpful, picked up his phone to let him know who had texted him, because he was running late and she thought it might be important for his work.

The text said, 'Good morning honey! I love you and I hope you have an awesome day—I'm so proud of you!' followed by the two-love-hearts-for-eyes emoji.

When Martin emerged from the ensuite, Heather calmly asked who the text was from, and Martin replied that it was 'just a girl from that course' he had done six months before, who wouldn't leave him alone. Heather, not being a complete moron, told Martin that he was free to be with bad-emoji-using girl. Martin, shocked and appalled at Heather's unreasonable refusal to believe his frankly ironclad cover story, packed a bag and left.

When the couple's two teenaged sons got home that night, they found all their father's stuff on the front porch, and Heather told them that Martin was moving out. One of their sons asked his mother if it was 'because of that chick Dad is always texting', and Heather said yes.

So, if you've cheated, you're going to have all kinds of cleaning up to do, and it will have years-long ramifications. Probably best not to do it in the first place, yeah?

Ages 7–10

At this age, kids will have opinions and ideas about why you're getting a divorce. They might be relieved, especially if the tension in the house is so thick you could see it on a Saturday morning (the worst fights always seem to happen on a Saturday morning, don't they?)

They'll also have friends whose parents are divorced, and it may well be a bit more normalised. However, chances are your kids will be very upset and possibly very angry, and the younger ones in this age group may not quite grasp what 'divorce' is, so they'll need a simple explanation as well.

Lots of online resources suggest you reassure your kid that the divorce is not their fault. We're not so sure about this bit. Why would your kids think the divorce was their fault? Isn't saying it's not suggesting that you think it might be? Why *would* it be their fault, anyway? Instead, it's important to listen to your kids and hear what they have to say. Mostly, they'll be concerned about how their lives are going to change, and where they'll be living, and when they'll see their other parent.

They'll also be concerned about you and their other parent, and they'll want to discuss the reasons why this is all happening. Ten-year-olds are pretty with it, and they all watch a million YouTube videos a week each, so you'll have to be prepared for some pretty intense discussions. Once again, give answers if you've got them, and be as reassuring and loving as you can be, given you're also going through a major life crisis.

Ages 10–14

This is a super tricky age. Kids this age are S-M-A-R-T (you can't spell-say things like W-H-E-R-E I-S T-H-E C-H-O-C-O-L-A-T-E anymore, curses, because they can spell) and they know a lot more than we sometimes give them credit for.

As with younger age groups, they want to know who's going to look after them (you and their other parent, hopefully), what the arrangements will be, where they're going to live and if they're going to stay in the same school.

As with the previous age group, it's okay not to have answers for all of this at this stage. What you can say is 'I don't know, honey, but we're going to figure it out together', and then really include them in the decisions you need to make, and the decisions their other parent needs to make. Ask them when they'd like to see their other parent, if they have any friends whose parents are divorced, and what they'd like from you at this point.

If they're very distressed (and this goes for other age groups too), find them someone to talk to—a child psychologist, an older friend that you and they both trust, and perhaps your parents if they have a close bond.

Try really hard not to send them away in these early days, even to your parents or on a sleepover—you're their primary attachment figure (probably) and they need to know you are close by. They're grieving too.

Ages 14–18

Teenagers are awesome. They are so much fun. They can also be the most monumentally annoying people in the entire world, and parenting a teenager as a sole parent is an epic lesson in letting go of the little things. If you've got a teenager, you know what we're talking about.

Having said that, this generation of kids are fantastic human beings. They are so lovely and accepting and we think the least racist or bigoted generation that has ever existed.

It's tempting to treat your teenagers like your friends and a shoulder to cry on when you're getting divorced. Try not to do this, although they probably already know what's going on. Lucy asked her fourteen-year-old to tell her how he thinks the news that your parents are divorcing should be conveyed, and he said, 'Just tell them the truth, they already know'.

Of course, teenagers this age will have very firm opinions on matters such as their living arrangements. Teenagers have their own busy and full social lives, and their schedules are almost always frantic.

Oftentimes, teens are not interested in traipsing back and forth between houses each week, especially if the parent with less time with the child lives a long way away, or out of reach of the child's social networks. A family law court won't expect a parent to physically force a child over the age of about twelve or fourteen to spend time with either parent but will expect you to encourage the child to go to see their other parent and maybe even give the child consequences for not going. At the very least, the court will take the child's opinion into account when making any orders. (And see Chapter 6 for more on this.)

If there are orders in place, it is important to remember that you have a positive obligation to comply with them. It is not enough to passively comply, you have to encourage your teen to see their other parent.

But don't forget that behind the bluster, sullenness or hysterics of teenagers, they are grieving the loss of their intact family and need lots of love and attention at this point, and lots of understanding, not to mention the space to be heard and to talk through how they're feeling. (The car is often a great place to get teens to open up, as no doubt you already know!)

The good news is that at this age, you can watch *Ant-Man* or *Guardians of the Galaxy* together while eating a pizza bigger than your head and try to forget the whole debacle, at least for the night.

Adult children

Telling your adult children that you're getting a divorce is no easier than telling your minor children. With more marriages ending at the twenty-year or so mark, it's becoming more common for divorce to impact on adult children, and as a parent, you'll want to support your kids through this time, and to have them support you as much as is appropriate.

The most important thing with adult kids is to make sure you don't put them in a position where they have to take sides. As is the case with younger children, your adult children love their other parent too.

Our advice here is to tell them the truth, and to invite their other parent to speak with them as well. Oftentimes, adult children, like teenagers, already know that their parents' marriage is rocky, and the news won't come as a surprise. That isn't to say it won't hurt them—it's easy for others to downplay the emotional impact of divorce on your adult kids, but it's still a fundamental change to their family unit, and they will be worried about you, their other parent, and how their family is forever altered.

A key challenge of divorcing with adult children is the organising of weddings, the arrival of grandchildren, and the fact that adult children are often still emotionally and financially dependent on their parents, well into their mid- (and late!) twenties.

It's not at all uncommon for adult children to still live at home, and for them to have front-row seats to the decision to end the marriage, which can be very stressful for the adult children as well as for you. It can also add a complexity to property settlements, which we'll discuss later in the book—there's no need to worry about all of that right at this juncture.

Extended family

There's a few ways to do this. In tight-knit families, news of a divorce can be devastating (this can especially be so in families that have strong religious values). In others, every man and his dog is divorced, and that's just the way marriages end, generally.

Your close family will probably know most of the details by this time. And so you can utilise your village to do your dirty work for you. Ask your siblings to tell your cousins, and your parents to tell your aunts and uncles. You can give your grandparents a call yourself, or get your mum to. (That's what we did!) Generally these are not hugely difficult conversations because your family of origin (the family you came from, not the family you made) will almost invariably take your side.

Sometimes, though, someone close to you will volunteer something ridiculously hurtful like 'I always knew he was too good-looking for you' or 'Well, you know she always did have a wandering eye!' These people are jerks and they've shown you who they are. Dismiss them as best you can and then immediately call your closest family of origin member for an epic moan-session.

Or, you can tell your extended friends and family the modern way, and change your relationship status from 'married' to 'single' on Facebook. Hey, it might be attention seeking but you can't say it's not *efficient*.

Case study—Marjorie and Elsa

Marjorie was Elsa's mum. When Elsa told Marjorie that she and David were getting a divorce, Marjorie told Elsa that Elsa had 'always been a terrible wife', and that she was 'surprised David hadn't left years ago, considering how dreadfully you cook and take care of your house'.

Elsa told Marjorie that in her opinion, Marjorie was in fact a complete witch, and then they didn't speak to each other for two years.

Elsa was right—Marjorie was a complete witch.

WORKSHEET 2
HOW I PLAN TO TELL MY CHILDREN ABOUT OUR SEPARATION

As we've mentioned before, part of sticking to plans is writing them down and committing to them. In the worksheet below, you can plan out how you'd like to address the issue of telling your kids about your separation, before you have to do it.

How I'm feeling	
What my former spouse wants	
How will I deal with the issue of infidelity (if any) as a reason my marriage is ending?	
What unique needs do my kid/s have that will affect how I tell them?	1. 2. 3. 4.
How do the ages of my children impact on the way in which I will tell them?	
Will my former spouse and I tell the children together?	
What setting will I/we choose?	

How will I look after myself while I'm passing on this news?	
What information do I really want my kid/s to understand or know?	
What plans do my former spouse and I have in relation to the care of the kid/s?	
Anything else?	

4

The first night without your children

The hideous reality of separation is that you often go from being a full-time parent and spouse in a busy household where you're so run off your feet you barely have time to pour yourself a glass of wine or grab another beer, to having swathes of alone time stretching ahead of you with no children to look after or spouse to talk to.

On the first night, and thereafter, it's really important that you have a plan of action to help you cope. Try to organise to have dinner with a close friend on the first night, or even invite your closest friends over for a movie night and watch a truly inappropriate-for-kids movie, along with having chocolate, wine from a box and an extra-pepperoni pizza (we know you spend your life eating margarita and ham and pineapple because that's what your kids like).

Try really hard not to drink too much, because tipsy people often wind up texting and making late-night phone calls to their exes, and you're better than that. But if you're not, and you do, don't worry. It's pretty much par for the course, and probably they deserve it. Just remember the texts could end up in an affidavit or application for a protection order. Again, it might be better to send the texts to your best friend or sister instead.

As hard as it is, there are upsides to having time away from your children, and as part of your promise to be really super kind to yourself, it's a good idea to find those upsides. It's another one of those things where it gets easier as time passes.

Oftentimes, the end of a relationship can be so soul-destroyingly toxic that you might find some sense of relief in being out of it, and to wake up peacefully on a Saturday morning after a blissful sleep-in. The sheer joy of having the whole bed to yourself also really can't be discounted.

As long as you know your children are safe with their other parent, try to use the time to do things that are super fun but also tough with kids in the house—like bleaching all your towels in the bathtub. (No? Just us? Really?)

The list below is a bunch of things you can do when you don't have your kids to help fill in those empty hours, especially in the beginning. You've very likely never had a lot of free time, and now is your chance to do the things you haven't had the opportunity to do before.

These things don't have to be expensive. We know that funds are probably the tightest they've ever been. The list below contains things that are either free or reasonably cheap.

- Going to the supermarket alone (this is *bliss*).
- Baking—if you're not much of a cook, start with easy stuff like simple sugar cookies. (Google it—they're great! And as a bonus, your children will think you're, like, amazing.)
- Lying in the sun reading the weekend papers.
- Gardening, even if you're really crap at it (this is also called 'weeding').
- Buying Ikea furniture without any in-store meltdowns from little people.
- Putting Ikea furniture together without any little people 'helping'.

- Going to the hairdressers without your partner calling every twenty minutes to ask, 'Are you done yet? How long is this taking?! The kids are driving me mental!'
- Getting a pedicure every now and again.
- Appreciating not having to drag your children around with you 24/7.
- Going for a really long walk.
- Getting a dog, and taking the dog for a walk.
- Going for a run.
- Going to parkrun on Saturday morning and meeting fantastic parkrunners (check it out at www.parkrun.com.au/).
- Taking up long-distance running. (Rebekah did this and is now taking on marathons and triathlons.)
- Going back to studying: for example, starting that post-grad degree that you always wanted to do.
- Joining the gym and taking up yoga. (Lucy tried this and she now accepts that she finds yoga really *boring*. She spent the whole time thinking about what she was going to have for lunch.)
- Being able to occasionally go out for Friday night drinks at work, or going out every second Friday (for example) if you so choose.
- Dating (and this is a whole new world of weird—for those of us who last dated in our twenties some years ago, the whole online dating thing is very strange).
- Talking to your closest friends on the phone without little people instantly demanding attention.
- Cleaning the whole house top to bottom and *having it stay that way* for at least twenty-four hours (even the Lego).

- Having a kid-free dinner party, even if it's pot luck.
- Going out to dinner with your siblings and/or your parents.
- Planning and making really great, yay-the-kids-are-home dinners.
- Doing your Christmas or birthday shopping really early and wrapping the presents just like Martha Stewart.
- Watching Netflix at 2 p.m.
- Going to visit your friends on the weekend and taking their kids cupcakes even though it's nearly dinnertime.
- Becoming active in a cause that you believe in, such as joining a political party or a charity or the parents and citizens group at your kids' school.
- Finding a new hobby, like bushwalking. (There are loads of bushwalking clubs around, in both the city and the country—google 'bushwalking club' and see what pops up.)
- Going to the movies with a girlfriend/old mate and eating all the popcorn.
- Finishing the week's laundry and then folding it while you watch a show your kids hate.

We found the most important thing has been to develop a plan for your kid-free and spouse-free weekends. Otherwise, it's very easy to take to aimlessly wandering around, watching all the other 'happy' families enjoying their weekends together. (In the early days, you will *hate* the sight of happy, intact families, with their smug smugness radiating from them.)

We always try to have one or two activities lined up (from the above list—although watching Netflix at 2 p.m. doesn't really require a huge level of detailed planning) so that we don't find ourselves crying into a (third) glass of wine on Saturday night, or opening and closing the kids' bedroom doors. (Tip: keep them closed when they're not home, at least in the first few months.)

'I'd kill to have some time away from my kids!' and other clueless comments

You'll find that some people will say things to you like 'Wow, it must be great having every other week/every other weekend without your kids! Mine drive me crazy on the weekends!' Or, 'Geez, my partner follows me around *all* weekend. It must be so blissful to have all that time to yourself!'

This can be really hurtful, because for lots of people, it's not great to suddenly be a part-time parent,[31] or to be single at a later stage of your life.

Phone calls or even FaceTime with toddlers are no substitute for tucking them in, mainly because toddlers and younger children have a very disconcerting habit of putting the phone down and wandering away, and don't otherwise grasp good phone manners.

Teenagers don't much want to talk on the phone either to their mum or dad, and so it's possible to go days where the most in-depth conversation you've had with your children consists of:

'How are you, honey?'

'Good.'

'How was school?'

'Good.'

'What are you up to today?'

'Nothing much.'

'Okay, honey, have a great day!'

''K, bye.'

If you have a toddler, the calls go like this:

'Hi, baby!'

'Hi, Mummy/Daddy!'

'How are you?'

'Good! Today I wented to the movies and then I ... BEEP BEEP BEEP.'

This is upsetting, and people who are happily married and have their children full time can't possibly understand the deep well of hurt that exists in the pit of your stomach when you haven't seen

31 You're *not* but sometimes it feels that way.

your kids in five days and there's still two more to go. We can't promise that it gets better, but with careful planning, it gets more manageable.

Case study—Jonathan and Seema

Jonathan and Seema separated after ten years of marriage. They had three children, aged six, four and two. Jonathan worked long hours but was a very good and hands-on father when he was home. Money was tight in the family and this had contributed to the end of the marriage, although they were still quite amicable.

Jonathan and Seema agreed that, as the children were so small and his hours were so long, the children would move with Seema into her parents' place, and that Jonathan would rent a nearby three-bedroom unit, in order to care for the children for two nights every second weekend. He would also see the children every Wednesday night for dinner at a local restaurant and care for them for half of school holidays.

Seema appeared to Jonathan to be thriving in her new life, and always had a lot of people around her, including her parents, and her sisters, nieces and nephews, while Jonathan felt very alone, and bereft without his children. It seemed to him that he was alone in his flat after work an awful lot.

Jonathon had always been very interested in politics, and so he joined the local branch of a political party, and took up indoor soccer. He also talked to Seema about what he could do to be more involved in the children's lives outside of their set time with him, and together he and Seema agreed he would take their two- and four-year-old to daycare three mornings a week, and go to school assembly with his oldest on Fridays.

In time, Jonathan felt much happier with his new circumstances.

One thing we have found, and that many of our friends have found, is that in a strange way, not having your children around

100 per cent of the time can actually make you an even better, more engaged parent when you do have them.

This is a bit of a taboo thing to admit in our society, especially for mothers, but having down time while your kids are being cared for by their other loving parent can become a real blessing. In our view, there's absolutely nothing wrong with that—what could be wrong with having two engaged, rested and loving separated parents instead of two angry, shouty parents who loathe each other but still live together?

The difficulties of being single after a long marriage

It's not always the case that a marriage ends when you have small children at home—in fact, as we've discussed, more and more marriages are ending around the twenty- and thirty-year mark, when the children have left home or are just about to. This carries with it unique and difficult issues all of their own, when you have to deal with the harsh reality of life as a single person after a long marriage.

One woman we know separated after a 28-year marriage when her three children were adults. We can assure you that the trauma is just as real at that time. After all, when you've been married for so long, you will have had very few weekends free of your children or a partner in that whole time. To find yourself in this situation can be quite devastating. It can be hard to know what to do with all that spare time.

The key to surviving these long and empty days is to fill them up again. The ideas above apply equally to you, and the worksheet below is just as important. Our friend who divorced after twenty-eight years says that somehow each day got just a little bit better. It did for her and it will for you.

Case study—Jan

Jan divorced her husband after thirty-three years of marriage. She was fifty-six and had never lived by herself. It had been a relatively good marriage but once her children left home she realised they had absolutely nothing to talk about and, frankly, every single thing he did annoyed the living daylights out of her.

The family home was sold, and Jan moved into a two-bedroom apartment in a master-built community. Her adult daughter lived nearby but Jan didn't see her, or her grandchildren, quite as much as she had expected.

Jan hadn't worked outside of her family's business throughout her marriage (she ran the books for her husband) but decided, after yet another lonely night when she drank too much pinot grigio by herself, that she would get a job.

The next day she saw a sign in the local newsagency advertising for a part-time office manager. Jan applied and to her surprise she got the job. She also spoke with her daughter and asked when it would be helpful for her to pick her granddaughters up from school, and was very happy when her daughter said that Fridays would be a lifesaver. This meant that on Fridays she picked up the kids, and then took them to flute lessons, and went back to her daughter's place, where she usually ended up staying for dinner.

Jan also joined the local swim group and boxercise class at the country club in her community, and made two good friends, and also an enemy, which was very interesting too.

She was still lonely from time to time but every day brought new challenges, especially as she learnt the world of work, and she felt herself growing as a person.

In Jan's case, what worked was finding new meaning in her life, and in order to do this she reached out to her community and her loved ones. We know you can do the same, and rediscover your own spark and joy.

WORKSHEET 3
THINGS I CAN DO WHEN I DON'T HAVE MY CHILDREN OR I'M BY MYSELF

As we've mentioned before, part of sticking to plans is to write them down and commit to them. In the worksheet below, you can list activities that you'd like to do during your childfree time, and make a plan to do them. It might seem silly but it can really help.

By doing this, you can hopefully avoid binge-watching Netflix while getting completely drunk on very cheap and nasty wine you found at the back of the cupboard after you'd finished all the good stuff.

Date	Activity	Did I do it? Was it fun?

5

The first month

We're a month in now. Hopefully by now you've stopped all of that sobbin', at least to the point where you can function semi-well again.

As a family lawyer, Rebekah finds many people tell her at this point that they are quite relieved the marriage is over, and just want it all sorted. For others, this is only the beginning of the grieving period. A friend of ours didn't really emerge from her pain cocoon until the four-month mark, probably because she was being trickle-truthed and finding out more about her husband's infidelity every day.

You may well find that you're more upset at this point than in the very beginning, because in the beginning you were in shock. This is totally normal and absolutely okay. You might also have experienced the divorce diet, where you lose huge amounts of weight without even trying. This is your body's reaction to stress and that's why it's so important to remember to be kind to yourself, and occasionally eat a burger (or two).

By now, you might have a clear idea about how you want your new life to look. You'll be starting to think about things like **parenting plans, consent orders**, and what the difference is (we'll come to all that very shortly).

Parenting plan—a written agreement signed and dated by parents and setting out parenting arrangements for children. It is not approved by or filed with a court and is not legally binding but the court will take notice of it. A parenting plan supersedes an earlier court order.

Consent order—an agreement between the parties (in family law generally about the children or finances) that is approved by the court and then becomes a legally enforceable court order.

You might have started filling in the property assets spreadsheet your lawyer has given you (more on this in Chapter 9), and you might have finally started sleeping a little better. You've probably had one or two weekends without the kids, or perhaps even longer, and you've survived them, even though it was pretty awful (or maybe not—maybe you've been pretty much a sole parent for years now, and you're very rightly relishing the break).

Or perhaps you're still in a complete state of shock (in other words, denial) and you might not have any idea what you want, or need, to do about your new reality. All this is totally fine and completely normal.

In this section we're going to talk about the *Family Law Act 1975*, which as we discussed earlier is an Act of the Australian Parliament. For most aspects of family law, the Family Law Act is the most important piece of legislation and it applies across Australia.[32] This means that if you've separated in Ballina or Ballarat, Brisbane or Burra, you're covered by the same laws.

You might be starting to get into the formal negotiations about your parenting plans and your property settlement, and you may have your first period conference (meeting) with your lawyer coming up. This is an important meeting and you'll need to spend some time preparing for it. The worksheet at the end of this chapter is a space for you to write down any questions you want to have answered at your first meeting, and also provides space for you to write down the answers you get.

32 Western Australia has its own Act, see pages 16–17 for more.

In this chapter we also answer some of the most common questions people have at their first conference that aren't purely legal but are often asked.[33]

First up—be the Sane Parent

Our dad, Tony, has been a family lawyer for nearly forty years, the poor man. So basically there's nothing he hasn't seen or heard. His best advice to both of us when we got divorced (within four months of each other! Divorce really can be catching) is to always be the Sane Parent.

He says that in almost every divorce with kids there's the Crazy Parent and there's the Sane Parent. Sometimes the Crazy Parent and the Sane Parent swap roles. Very occasionally you get one of those beautiful divorces where both the parents are Sane Parents. More often, you get two Crazy Parents and they're often the cases that end up in years-long court battles.

Being the Sane Parent is hard work. It means not acting like a crazy person, which sounds easy but actually isn't. It's about taking the moral high ground and not sending mad text messages every time your ex annoys you. You'll hear the phrase 'child-focused' a lot in family law, and that's basically what being the Sane Parent is. It's being focused on your child and not on your trench war with your ex.

Instead of spending your precious time fighting with your ex, be the parent who gets the kids to school on time, who has clean uniforms for them, who polishes their shoes and does their home reading, who pays child support on time, who turns up to collect them on time, who drops them off on time, who goes to school functions and parent–teacher interviews, who has food in the fridge and clean dishes in the cupboard, who remembers dentist appointments, who takes them to the beach or the pool on hot days, who doesn't use them as a messenger or as a spy, who drives them to footy practice or to ballet, who remembers sunscreen and hats and water bottles, who cuddles and kisses them goodnight. Be the parent who meets their needs.

33 Think of all the money you're saving by not having to ask your lawyer this stuff!

Being the Sane Parent means you have to really consider your own motivations in your interactions with your ex when it comes to the kids. During a dispute with your ex (over changing access days or consenting to ears being pierced or whatever), ask yourself if you're being difficult for the sake of being difficult, or because you don't want to give your ex what they want on a particular point. If someone else was asking the same thing, would you take the same approach? It can be really hard to take a step back and consider whether or not the fight you're having is really about the issue at hand, or if it's really about your possibly-decades-long resentment and anger. If it's the latter, that's where you get to practise being the Sane Parent! Lucky you!

In cases where both parents are acting badly, judges often have an opinion, which is published to the world, although the names are anonymised (as in, the parties are given made-up names). In one matter, the judge commented, 'I am not in a position to make any finding about most of the facts but they do indicate a completely dysfunctional and uncooperative arrangement between two parents who have a great love for the child but whose focus is on anyone other than him'.[34]

It is very easy to get to the point where the relationship between you and your ex deteriorates so badly that comments like this are made by judges in court decisions. Nobody wants to read that a judge thinks they have completely dropped the ball when it comes to being child-focused. And you really do not want to hear a judge say that the risk of harm to your child of staying in your care due to your unrelenting hatred of the other parent outweighs the benefit of a relationship with you. Judges have and will continue to make these sorts of decisions, although fortunately very rarely.

We promise you that even on the darkest days of sole parenting, all children respond to stability, and love, and boundaries, and that if you are the Sane Parent, and you raise your children in a happy home full of warmth and care, you'll be repaid in spades as your child grows older.

With a bit of luck your ex will read this book too and will also decide to be the Sane Parent. All the better! When you're both Sane

34 Penski & Kocher [2013] FamCA 255

Parents, the only losers are your divorce lawyers. After all, it's about loving your children more than you hate your ex (so sometimes you've really, really, *really* got to love your children).

The pitfalls of social media

As we all know, Facebook, Twitter and Instagram, Snapchat and LinkedIn (and that's all we know about, sorry) are great ways to stalk your ex, or send subliminal messages to them and all your friends and family about how awesomely you're doing. They are also great ways to really get yourself in trouble when it comes to your family law matter or your property matter.

That new boat you've just bought? That's going in an affidavit. Your rant about how you're going to turn your kids against their other parent because the deadbeat loser hasn't paid child support/dropped the kids off/remembered Billy's shoes, again? That's going in an affidavit. Your private posts on your private single parents' group? Affidavit. You blind drunk at the club with your buddies? You can bet that's going in the affidavit.

Assume that everything you post on social media will be screenshot and sent to your ex. It's a small world and six degrees of separation is more like three in Australia. Assume that your high school friend's best friend is your ex's new partner's sister and that they are dutifully sending screenshots of every single thing you post online to your ex.

Trust us on this—it happens. It happens every day. And it all winds up in an affidavit, meaning you then have to explain to the judge why you didn't mean that/didn't buy that/didn't say that. The worst example Rebekah has seen was a self-represented litigant who posted an expletive-filled rant on Facebook—about the judge in her case. You can bet that went in the affidavit.

You must also be aware that it's against the law to publish any details identifying anyone involved in a family law court matter, including children. This means that you cannot post anything on Facebook or other social media about your case, and it's very likely the judge will find out if you do, and you'll have a lot of difficult explaining to do.

Dealing with your lawyer

A common refrain from people involved in family law matters is that their lawyer is hard to deal with, hard to contact, and hard to fire if needs be. Lawyers can be intimidating people and most people don't have to deal with us very often. (And yes, we get told lawyer jokes all the time. Our personal favourite is: 'What do you call 100 lawyers at the bottom of a pool?' Answer: 'A good start.')

In this section, we're going to talk a little more about the relationship you'll have with your lawyer, how to get the most out of your precious time and money, and how to resolve disputes if they arise throughout your matter.

What should I expect in my first conference with my lawyer?

As we've said before, it's very important to remember that your lawyer is not your therapist or your counsellor. They're about $400 an hour more, for starters.

It's a very common thing for a newly separated person to cling to their lawyer as a life raft in a scary sea full of sharks. But your lawyer is one of the sharks, too. It's our job to represent you to the best of our ability, but we're guns for hire, not your friend (sorry).

It can be helpful to take one of your actual friends (or your mum or dad, sister or brother) with you as a support person to your first conference with your lawyer. This will be fine with your lawyer, they're quite used to it.

There's often a lot to take in and your support person can take down detailed notes, which you won't be able to do because you'll be concentrating on what's being said, and asking and answering questions. You'll be able to ask your support person later what was said or what the lawyer asked you to do in case you forget—easy to do if you're stressed and anxious—which is a lot cheaper than having to ask your lawyer for the same information again.

To give you some idea of costs, lawyers bill in six-minute units. This means that for every six minutes they're working on your matter (or your 'file') they will charge it to your bill. This includes:

- reading your emails
- replying to your emails
- taking your phone calls
- returning your phone calls
- leaving you a voicemail message
- listening to your voicemail messages
- talking to your ex's lawyer
- emailing your ex's lawyer
- settling documents with your ex's lawyer
- representing you in court
- travelling to and from court (some lawyers will charge travel fees—before you sign it check your costs agreement to see if yours does!)
- attending conferences with you
- taking your statement for your affidavit
- drafting your affidavit
- amending your affidavit after you change it
- printing off any documents
- drafting any document.

The best way to get value out of your visits with your lawyer, particularly the first visit, is to be prepared. When a client has absolutely no idea when their kids were born (which happens more than you might think!), how much their home is worth, how much is owing on the mortgage, or who their super is with, time is wasted, which then translates to more costly meetings being required in the future.

To help with this, your lawyer will probably ask you to fill in an intake sheet before your appointment. This is to save time in the appointment, as the sheet will ask for things like your name, address and date of birth, and those of your former partner and the kids. The intake sheet ensures that most of the basic information is given to your lawyer in a timely (and legible) way. To further save time and stress, some law firms send the intake sheet out to clients by email before the appointment.

In order to get the most out of your meeting, bring the following documents:

- Your most up-to-date superannuation statement. (Your super fund can email you the most recent one if you can't find it, or can talk you through how to log on and download it.)
- A market appraisal of the home. (Ask a local real estate agent, who will usually do it for free.)
- Your three latest tax returns and notices of assessment.
- Statements or transaction histories for every account that you hold with a financial institution (including the mortgage). Bring the latest copies but be prepared for your lawyer to ask you for six months' worth or more, particularly if there are allegations of misuse of funds.
- A rough valuation (from an online site such as www.redbook.com.au) of your car, motorcycle and/or boat.
- Details of any shares or interests in companies and trusts, including values if possible.
- Child support assessment if there has been one.

As an aside, it's often a very upsetting moment when you get a letter from your lawyer saying:

> Dear Mr/Mrs Jones,
>
> RE: In the matter of Jones & Jones
> Blah blah blah, unintelligible gobbledegook.

Yours sincerely
John Brown
Solicitor[35]

It can be really confronting realising that your 'matter' now has a formal name that your lawyer and your ex's lawyer talk about in very formal terms, and that the name of the matter is your name versus your ex's name. It's something that you have to prepare yourself for as you dive into this strange world. Believe us, though, that it's not as upsetting as having the name of your matter written as 'your assault charge'. You do not want to end up there, which is why we don't send nasty texts to our exes, which can escalate to, well, assault.

Getting back to business, there's a duty to make full and frank disclosure of financial circumstances in family law matters, so your lawyer may ask you to provide more documents, depending on your situation.

If you have never done the banking, then go into your bank and ask them to give you the current statements. Also ask them to set you up with internet banking because in your new life as a single person, you will need to be able to do your own banking. You will probably have a new sense of empowerment as you masterfully navigate your own finances, like the boss you are.

Your lawyer will also go through with you the parenting arrangements that are in place now (if any), how they are working, how the kids are coping and how the communication between you and your ex is going. As family dispute resolution is compulsory unless there is family violence, child abuse or a matter of urgency (like an impending relocation or abduction), they will probably go through the family dispute resolution process with you, and let you know what your BATNA and WATNA is.[36]

BATNA is 'Best Alternative To a Negotiated Agreement' and is basically your best day in court where you get everything you want.

35 Obviously this is often also very upsetting if you have a different name to your former spouse, but we couldn't make that work stylistically.

36 Roger Fisher and William Ury, *Getting to Yes: Negotiating an Agreement without Giving In*, 1981, Simon and Schuster.

WATNA is 'Worst Alternative To a Negotiated Agreement' and so is your worst day in court where there is no doubt at the end of the day that you really lost that one. Any agreement should sit somewhere in the middle of your BATNA and WATNA.

Of course, the great advantage of negotiating your own agreement is that you and your ex know better than anyone the exact time it takes to get child one to ballet and child three to soccer on the same day, during peak-hour traffic (which seems to now start at 1 p.m. in Brisbane and possibly does not actually end in Sydney).

For property matters, your lawyer will want to work with you to establish:

- What the property pool is—that is, what you and your ex (either together or separately or even with other people) own now.
- Contributions—that is what you and your ex had at the beginning of the relationship, what you both earned during the relationship and possibly post-separation, any substantial gifts, compensation payments or inheritances received, renovations done, work done for a family business and time spent as a stay-at-home parent.
- Future needs—the age and state of health of both parties, any disparity of income, care of children and any need for retraining after being a stay-at-home parent.

Generally speaking—and you should get legal advice specifically for your own matter if you can—the contributions of a stay-at-home parent or a parent working part time equal the contributions of a full-time earner.

So when you tell your lawyer that your ex told you that you will not get anything because all you have done is stay at home with the kids, do not be surprised if your lawyer rolls their eyes (at least mentally). It's not true, not even the tiniest little bit. We'll talk more about this later in the book.

What is a costs agreement?

A costs agreement is a document that your lawyer must legally give to you. It sets out all the information regarding what and how your lawyer will charge you, who will look after your matter (in other words, which lawyer), what your lawyer will do, what you need to do, and circumstances where you can fire each other.

What is a trust account and why does my lawyer want money for it?

A trust account is where solicitors have to put money that their clients have paid to them on account of future fees and outlays. Sometimes the proceeds of a sale of a home will also be held in the trust account until there is an agreement on how these proceeds will be divided.

Most lawyers will want money up front because family law clients are notorious for not paying their lawyers. Family law clients are often very keen that a lawyer do the work immediately, but then once the dust has settled, are less than keen to pay for that work. Family lawyers have come to recognise this and have realised that the best way to go out of business is to not get funds in trust first, because even though lawyers seem really, really expensive (and they are), they are also usually (especially in family law) small businesses with their own bills to pay.

Lawyers are so expensive because being a lawyer is expensive—it costs about $50 000 in tertiary fees just to become a lawyer, and we have to pay our staff wages, and pay rent, gas and electricity bills, huge professional insurance and membership fees, not to mention our car leases—Mercedes don't come cheap, after all![37]

Solicitors' trust accounts are very strictly regulated and solicitors cannot just use the money however they like. Solicitors can only deal with funds from trust if there is a **court order**, written agreement of the owners of the funds or a bill has been given to the client and the client has not queried the bill within seven days. Solicitors who misuse trust funds can and are sent to jail, because it's stealing.

37 Joking, just joking. We drive Volvos.

Court order—the actions the parties or a party must do to carry out a decision made by a court. An order may be either interim or final. Interim means that it's not yet finalised, but must be followed until it is finalised.

What do I do when I'm unhappy with my lawyer?

Lawyers are only human. Your lawyer, if they're good at their job and respected within the profession, will be busy. They'll be in court a lot. They'll be uncontactable for huge chunks of time. When you're a lawyer and you're in court, you can't play on your phone (worse luck), you can't answer emails, you can't duck out to take a quick call. You have to sit in front of the judge either listening or talking for hours and hours at a time and that's it. In this hyper-connected world of instant communication it feels like torture for us and seems almost inexplicable to our clients.

However, despite understanding all this, you might feel like your lawyer:

- avoids your calls and doesn't update you enough
- thinks your matter is too small and unimportant to bother about
- is just too busy to deal with your matter
- makes things too complicated and you can't understand half of what they say
- doesn't understand how awful all this is for you
- is dragging the matter on and is way too expensive.

While all or some of this may be true, a lot of these issues can be resolved, and we'll talk more now about how you can resolve them.

The most common complaints made about lawyers involve clients who are unsatisfied with the outcome of their matter; clients who feel they have been overcharged, and clients who actually have been overcharged; and delays and rudeness.

Sometimes lawyers, like other professionals, fail to meet their client's expectations. A key skill for a lawyer is managing expectations, so that clients understand what is likely to occur in their matter. Be cautious if a lawyer promises that you will 'win'. In property settlement matters the outcome must be 'just and equitable'. In parenting matters the outcome must be 'in the best interests of the child/ren'. Family law is not about 'winning' or even about justice. This can be a very bitter pill to swallow.

Some lawyers overcharge vulnerable clients or even steal their money from the trust account. This seriously infuriates other lawyers who do the right thing. If you feel that you have been overcharged, speak up; and if your lawyer does not provide itemised bills, you can ask for one.

An itemised bill sets out exactly what you have been charged for: each email, letter, telephone call, court appearance and drafted document. Rebekah sends out itemised bills as a matter of course in family law matters, as the costs add up and it is important that clients can see exactly how those costs have been tallied.

If you notice an error on a bill—for example, a telephone call that you know from your own phone records took six minutes has been billed at an hour—let your lawyer know. They will most likely be extremely grateful that you picked the error up and will probably be more careful about using the timer function on their time-recording system in future.

Delays can be frustrating because this is probably the most awful thing that you have ever been through. But for your lawyer, it's just another case, and there can be reasons for delays. Your lawyer may not communicate with you unless there is something to tell you. Lawyers are acutely aware that legal services cost money, so we generally keep that in mind and avoid unnecessary communication, which often has the effect of really annoying our clients when we're actually only trying to do the right thing. (Your invitation to our pity-party is in the mail, along with our bill.)

Sometimes lawyers 'triage' cases, so they may be focused on a trial and not focusing on yours. Of course, this isn't perfect, but really, you do want a lawyer who has experience and who actually goes to court. The downside to having a lawyer who knows what they are doing is that they sometimes get bogged down in trial preparation, to the detriment of their communication with their other clients (the words 'trial prep' can strike fear into the hearts of lawyers).

If you do have a problem or a concern about how things are going, raise it with your lawyer. They'll appreciate you being frank with them about any concerns you have and will welcome the opportunity to try to resolve them.

We suggest you send a brief email succinctly outlining your issue in neutral language (so, not 'you're an overcharging jerk and you wear ugly ties') and ask if your lawyer could let you know how they intend to address your issue. For example, if you feel that your lawyer is taking too long to return your phone calls, you could ask what would be a reasonable time period in which you could expect a return call. Or if you feel that your legal bills are piling up and you see no end in sight, you could ask for an overview of the strategy to resolve the matter, and for advice on what can be done to reduce the fees.

In the vast majority of cases, an open dialogue between you and your lawyer can resolve the issue without having to take it any further.

What if I have to make a formal complaint about my lawyer?

The simple truth is that sometimes matters will be mishandled. The legal profession is, sadly, pretty susceptible to psychological issues. It can be a tough job, especially in areas like family law where lawyers are dealing with vulnerable people, overloaded courts and high stakes.

Many of the disciplinary cases against lawyers involve otherwise good lawyers who have, for whatever reason, basically dropped their bundle. The outcome for their clients can be devastating. Most firms voluntarily run programs such as enhanced management reviews, to monitor their lawyers so that any slips are picked up and dealt with quickly.

Solicitors have to follow the Australian Solicitors' Conduct Rules and these set out things like not communicating with another lawyer's client, not being rude and not lying to the court.[38]

If you cannot resolve your complaint with your lawyer, there are Legal Services Commissions in each state. According to the Queensland Legal Services Commission, common complaints about lawyers involve:

- lack of communication, or rudeness
- delays
- costs
- liens (a legal practitioner's right to keep a client's property until they pay the legal practitioner's fees and disbursements).[39]

These are categorised as 'consumer disputes' and are generally dealt with by mediation or through the regulatory authority.

Other complaints involve serious breaches of a solicitor's ethical duties, which can be classified as unsatisfactory professional conduct or professional misconduct. If a solicitor has behaved unethically, they can be prosecuted and disciplined, and struck off the roll of lawyers, which means they can't practise as a lawyer anymore.

The websites for the various commissions around the country are:

- Legal Services Commission Queensland: www.lsc.qld.gov.au
- Office of the Legal Services Commissioner New South Wales: www.olsc.nsw.gov.au
- Victorian Legal Services Board and Commissioner: www.lsb.vic.gov.au
- Legal Services Commission of South Australia: www.lsc.sa.gov.au

38 www.lawcouncil.asn.au/policy-agenda/regulation-of-the-profession-and-ethics/australian-solicitors-conduct-rules.

39 www.lsc.qld.gov.au/complaints/types-of-complaints.

- Legal Practice Board of Western Australia: www.lpbwa.org.au/Home.aspx
- Legal Profession Board of Tasmania: www.lpbt.com.au
- In the Northern Territory, complaints against solicitors are handled by the NT Law Society: www.lawsocietynt.asn.au.

How to sack your lawyer

The decision to sack your lawyer is a big one.

Firstly, you should try to resolve the issue with your lawyer directly, as we've discussed above. This can be hard because some lawyers are difficult to get hold of, difficult to talk to, and difficult to make understand your concerns. Perhaps your lawyer is just too busy for your matter, or never returns your calls, or is frankly just too expensive as your matter drags on. Or perhaps your lawyer has had a mental breakdown (it happens).

If you've tried to resolve the issue, and you feel like your lawyer isn't representing you as you would like, you can sack your lawyer. The easiest way is to find a new lawyer and they will send your old lawyer your authority to release the file. Your old lawyer does not always have to do this until your account with them is paid. You do not need to speak to your old lawyer; your new lawyer can handle the changeover.

If you chop and change your lawyer more times than you change your underwear, you can expect that your matter will not proceed particularly smoothly, as your new lawyer will need time to read through your matter and get up to speed. Your new lawyer will most probably also have to charge you for reading documents that your old lawyer has already charged you for reading or drafting. The other side in your dispute, or the judge, could also start making comments about your capacity to give instructions.

This isn't to say that you shouldn't sack your lawyer, just that it's an important decision that can have a negative impact on your matter if you don't tread carefully.

Separated under one roof

Being forced by finances to stay living under the one roof while you go through a sales process or because you simply can't afford to sell right now is becoming more and more common. However, proving that you've actually separated under one roof can be a bit tricky. To demonstrate to the court that you've been separated under one roof for the period of time that you say you've been, you need to provide a sworn statement (an affidavit). In your statement you'll need to show:

- a change in sleeping arrangements (i.e. you stopped sleeping in the same bed)
- a change in how you conduct family outings (i.e. you stopped going on date nights together)
- a change in your joint finances (i.e. you got separate bank accounts or otherwise divided your finances)
- you told people such as your family and friends, and/or Facebook, that you've separated
- a good reason why you continued to live in the same house (i.e. you had the house on the market and couldn't afford to move out until it sold)
- any arrangements you made for children under the age of eighteen
- if you've advised any other government agencies, such as Centrelink, of your separation.

Sometimes former couples remain separated under one roof for months or even years. If you've got a big house and you're relatively amicable, it can work well. Rebekah has had clients who have been separated for years and years and have only finalised their split when the kids have grown up, because they were quite good mates and neither wanted to miss out on a single moment with their kids. These people deserve sainthoods as well as a divorce. Most of us aren't these people.

My ex won't move out of the house—can I have the police remove them?

This can be a terrible situation. It can be difficult to live as a separated couple under the same roof, but unless there is domestic violence the police will tell you that it's a family law matter not a police matter, and that you should see your lawyer.

The question of whether to move out or not can be a tough one. If there is any question of violence, or if the children are being exposed to violence (including verbal abuse), then move. There is no magic in staying—you do not forfeit the home or any part of the home if you move, and with a shocking number of Australian women killed each year by their domestic partner, it could be the difference between life and death. All too often violence erupts under these circumstances.

Who ends up with the home, or whether it is sold, is just one of a whole host of matters to sort out. If you move out, there can be the danger that the other party refuses to allow the home to be sold without a court order forcing the matter, but this would probably happen anyway whether you stay or move out.

Separation can be very tough, even when you're not in a financially precarious position, and the thought of being separated and homeless can be too much for many people to contemplate. Get legal advice early and your lawyer can start negotiating with your ex or their lawyer about whether your ex buys you out of the house, or if the house is to be sold, or some other just and equitable division occurs.

If you do move out and the other party refuses to, speak to your lawyer as a matter of priority about whether you should stop paying the mortgage or if you need a caveat over the sale of the house, if the house is in their sole name. Don't take any steps (like stopping your mortgage payments) until you speak to your lawyer (and see Chapter 9 for more on this).

'My ex is a narc' and other armchair diagnoses

If you can, try to resist the urge to diagnose your ex-spouse with a mental health problem. The vast majority of separated people armchair-diagnose their exes with narcissistic personality disorder, bipolar, or some other Cluster B personality disorder, and it's usually not the case. It's just that divorce brings out the absolute worst in everyone, and it's really hard to accept that the person who you promised to love until death, who's seen you give birth, or who you've seen give birth, could be so absolutely horrible to you when you're so lovely! They must be mad. In fact, they must have some deep-seated psychological problem, right?

Probably not. If they're otherwise functional, and their disordered behaviour is something that's new (and started around the time you separated), then it's more than likely their reaction to stress.

One of the things that might be useful to try to remember is that even though your ex is being so incredibly hurtful to you, they're also very hurt themselves, even if they're the ones doing the leaving. The thought of leaving your partner is often much more attractive than the actual reality of leaving your partner—the grass always seems greener on the other side.

If your ex has been quite revolting for the last year or longer and then suddenly leaves, this could be because they have been going through their stages of grief about leaving the relationship. Although it might feel like a double slap in the face—after all, you've put up with their moods, withdrawn nature and nastiness for them to just suddenly leave—if you accept that it is all part of this crazy thing called the human condition, then you will be able to start to process your own grief and loss.

So you can be assured that no matter how much of a brave face they're putting on, it's tough for them as well. They think you're being an absolute monster, too (which you're not, you're delightful).

As hard as it is, trying to be as kind as you can—if only for your children's sakes—can pay dividends (and not just in your property settlement). You catch more flies with honey than with vinegar (and yes, in this little tale, your ex is the fly).

Often Rebekah will be faced with a client or client's ex trying to run a case that the other parent is crazy, dangerous and evil, but the person making these allegations is seeking shared care—as if somehow the other parent is crazy, but for only half the time. If you want shared care or for your kids to live with their other parent for half the school holidays, then it is going to be hard for anyone to accept your armchair diagnosis that the other parent is an axe-wielding homicidal maniac.

Some exes, however, are fully-fledged disordered people. Statistics are in short supply, but estimates are that about 5 per cent of the general population have some kind of Cluster B personality disorder. You will know they're disordered because they were disordered before you decided to separate—in fact, their disorder is one of the prime reasons your marriage has ended. It is generally only safe to say that someone has a personality disorder or a mental health challenge if they've been diagnosed with one by someone credentialled to make that diagnosis—that someone being a medical professional.

In such cases, it's crucial that you get very good support from a psychologist who's knowledgeable about treating the partners and ex-partners of people who have personality disorders. Being divorced from a disordered person is enough to make you go legitimately crazy yourself, and it's very easy to fall into the trap of bending over backwards to accommodate them, and in doing so, fail to look after yourself. It's really hard to emotionally disengage from such people, but not buying into their drama and disorder is one of the best weapons in your arsenal. No contact, as far as is humanly possible, can be your friend and your key to a drama-free life.

My ex is abusive. What are my options here?

If you have any reason to fear your ex, you must seek urgent help. Leaving a relationship is the most dangerous time for a woman—we don't say that to upset men (#NotAllMen et cetera), we say it because it's true.

Abuse is:

- Physical assaults: for example, choking (which is a major predictor of further attempts to murder, and of actual murder, and must be taken extremely seriously), beatings, pushing and threatening harm.

- Acts of sexual violence, forced sex or forcing someone to do sexual acts they don't wish to do.
- Emotional, such as name-calling and put-downs, disrespectful treatment.
- Isolation from supports, family and community, or using family and community to intimidate. This can include sending texts or posting on Facebook.
- Stalking or monitoring 'every move', including stalking on the internet, through social media, or the use of GPS tracking devices.
- Psychological, such as blaming the person being abused for the behaviour; telling the person being abused that they have mental health problems or anxiety disorders; manipulating or deliberately twisting reality; moving personal belongings or furniture and then denying that this has been done; and denying that the abusive behaviour occurred.
- Financial, such as denying living expenses or providing only meagre 'housekeeping money'; preventing someone from working; manipulating the child support system; intimidating someone into signing legal and financial documents that put them in debt; standing over someone to demand money.
- Preventing someone from practising their spirituality or faith, or forcing them to adopt a faith or spirituality that is not their own.
- Harming or threatening to harm loved ones, including children.
- Harming or threatening to harm pets.
- Legal, such as exploiting the family law system to intimidate, exhaust, exploit or disempower someone.[40]

---

40 Excerpted from 'Domestic and Family Violence: What Is It and Where Do I Find Support?', www.1800respect.org.au/get-help/common-questions/what-is-domestic-family-violence.

There is a lot of help at hand if you need to get away from an abusive ex (man or woman). You need very good legal advice (start with Legal Aid if you don't have a lot of money) and you can also access a refuge if you need a safe, secure place to stay (and yes, refuges take children).

See Resources for more, but make sure you check out the federal government's website on safely leaving an abuser (www.1800respect.org.au), which has access to telephone counselling (phone: 1800 737 732) and online counselling, and help is available 24/7.

At the same time, if your lawyer ever tells you to make up allegations of abuse in order to 'win' against your ex, fire that lawyer and report them to the Legal Services Commission in your state or territory (and see pages 74–5 for these). Lying in court or in sworn statements is a criminal offence and it's also, frankly, deeply immoral and damaging to your kids to make up stuff like this.

Economic abuse

Economic abuse is an insidious form of abuse. A recent survey has shown that 11 per cent of Australians have experienced some form of economic abuse in their lifetime. It can include:

- limiting your ability to access money (for example, giving you 'housekeeping' money that doesn't cover the cost of running your household)
- making you work in the family business, unpaid
- refusing to let you work outside of the home, or sabotaging your attempts to do so (for example, refusing to equally share in pick-ups and drop-offs of children when you are working, intentionally making you late to work, refusing you the opportunity to go to networking events or training, refusing to allow you time to study)
- cutting off your access to internet banking services by changing passwords

- refusing you access to bills or other expenses, so you don't know where money is going
- taking your pay to cover household expenses while spending all 'their' money on themselves
- a gambling problem, which greatly limits the financial resources available to the family
- a spending problem, where unnecessary items that the family income can't afford are frequently purchased.

The Commonwealth Bank of Australia has released a useful guide to 'Addressing Financial Abuse', which can be accessed here: www.commbank.com.au/content/dam/commbank/assets/about/opportunity-initiatives/addressing-financial-abuse-guide.pdf. Achieving a measure of financial freedom and self-control can be a crucial step in leaving an abusive relationship, and working through this guide can give you the tools to better understand and manage your finances post-separation.

Changing your will, power of attorney and the beneficiary of your super

If there's one thing worse than divorce, it would probably be dropping dead and your ex trying to get all your money or super because you didn't get around to changing your will or the beneficiary of your super. Although, you'll be dead, so you won't know about it to be annoyed about it. But just to be on the safe side, make sure you talk to your lawyer about changing your will, your enduring power of attorney and the beneficiary of your super.

Your enduring power of attorney is the legal document that sets out who can make decisions about your finances and/or health care if you're incapacitated (in a coma, have failing cognitive health, or become catastrophically brain damaged). You might not want your ex to be in the position where they literally have the choice to pull the plug on you.

If you don't have a lawyer, it's quite easy to do your own will, and many community groups, such as the Salvation Army, hold wills days where a volunteer solicitor will help you write or update your will. Some lawyers also have free wills days because it's a good way to get new clients in the door. A quick google of 'wills' will point you in the right direction. (But be really careful of those do-it-yourself will kits—wills are complex legal documents and if they can't be properly executed it can cost your beneficiaries—who are probably your kids or close family—a lot of money to sort out. It's really easy to make mistakes with DIY wills but those same mistakes are very difficult to fix.)

The Reconciliation Unicorn

There's a website called Chump Lady (www.chumplady.com), and if you're dealing with infidelity, you absolutely must check her out. She pulls no punches, and her advice is incredibly empowering. One of her themes is around reconciliation and how true reconciliation is as rare as unicorns.

At the one-month mark, as you prepare to really formalise your separation, you may be tempted to try to reconcile with your ex. You may have, in fact, reconciled once (or twice, or three times) before you got to the most recent split.

Divorce is sucky. Divorce is tough. Divorce is hard to follow through on. One man we know told his wife (and parents, and extended family) that he wanted a divorce, and then didn't even manage to make it through that same afternoon before going back home to beg for a second chance. The notion of reconciling will absolutely float through your mind, and there's absolutely nothing wrong with that.

And look, if you think you've both faced some hard truths and you've committed to couples counselling, and you both want to, why not try reconciling? The sad truth is, however, that it's statistically unlikely to stick. The reasons you split in the first place aren't going to go away, and now they'll be compounded by what you or your spouse did or said (or even slept with) while you were separated. If you are going to try to reconcile, the most important thing is, of course, your children and how you manage the transition back to being a couple.

The internet wisdom on reconciliation seems to be just common sense—take it slow, take time to date one another (away from your children if you have any), don't move straight back in together, and get lots of marriage counselling. Be absolutely truthful about anything that occurred during your separation that your spouse could be upset about—such as if you slept with anyone else, ran up huge debts, or told your mother your spouse's deepest, darkest secrets. Seek help from a counsellor if you have something like this to 'confess' to—it can really derail things if you blurt it out of the blue, or, worse, your spouse finds out about it some other way.

Legally, you can split up and get back together as many times as you want, as Australia doesn't have separation agreements—it's only when you file for divorce that it becomes a bit trickier. (Although our dad had one couple who got back together on the courthouse steps, so it does happen!)

Case study—Emma and Ahmed

Emma and Ahmed had been married for six years when they first separated. They had three children, all under five, and life was busy and strained in their household. Emma found herself falling in love with another man who she worked with, Anthony. Emma decided to leave Ahmed to pursue her relationship with Anthony.

Six months later, she asked Ahmed for a second chance. The reality of life as a single mother was very different than she had expected, and things weren't quite so exciting with Anthony now that there was no need to sneak around and stay in luxurious hotels together under the pretext of 'travelling for work'.

Ahmed agreed to giving their marriage another go, and she and the children moved back in with him, but within a year, the cracks were starting to show. They hadn't sought marriage counselling, and Ahmed couldn't forgive Emma for her affair. As he learnt more about Emma and Anthony's relationship, such as the fact that they had frequently gone away on weekends together while he looked after the children, he found himself increasingly angry and hurt. As a result, after eighteen months, he ended the marriage, this time for good.

So yes, you'll be tempted to give your marriage another go, and that's completely normal and par for the course. As family lawyers, it's common for us to see the same client come in two, three, or even four times before they're truly done.

It's also common for the new girlfriend to make an appointment about her boyfriend's divorce, and then for her 'separated' boyfriend to not turn up.[41] Rebekah doesn't accept these appointments anymore because almost invariably the 'separated' man has gone back to his wife once reality sets in. If he wants an appointment, he has to ring and make it himself.

My ex wants the kids to meet the new partner—what can I do?

To be frank, if your children are spending time with their other parent, there's precious little you can do to control who else they spend time with. If it's the Other Man or the Other Woman, this can understandably send you into a rage, but there's nothing you can do about it, except make your displeasure known, which is usually an exercise in futility.

If it's been three weeks and your ex has already hooked up with the newest love of their life, and wants to introduce them to the kids, again, there's not much you can do or say—the law won't intervene unless you have some really good reasons, such as pictorial evidence of rampant drug abuse (and even then it will be a long, drawn-out process).

Ultimately, within reason your ex can have anyone they like around your kids. Some websites advise that you insist on meeting anyone who will spend time with your kids, and while that's all fine in theory, there's really no need, and certainly no legal need. Your

41 This situation almost never plays out the other way round (as in, the new boyfriend calls to try to make an appointment for his still-married girlfriend with a divorce lawyer). We don't really know why, but it doesn't.

ex isn't legally obligated to let you meet the new lover, and so if they don't want you to, you can insist until the cows come home for all the good it will do you. Frankly, we'd wait until the relationship got a bit more serious before we inflicted such a thing on ourselves.

Also, one person's wish to 'check' that the new love is not a crazy person is another person's stalking. Oftentimes nothing good will come from such a meeting and we see all too often protection orders and even assault charges arising from them. At the very least, it will be excruciatingly awkward.

Established wisdom (so, Dr Phil) says that you should wait six months until you introduce your new partner to your kids. Steve Harvey (who wrote a book on dating called *Act Like a Lady, Think Like a Man*, so we guess that makes him an expert) says that that's nonsense—what if your kids hate them or they hate your kids? What if they secretly despise children and you've wasted six months on a relationship that can go nowhere?

Experts online vacillate between the two positions, so our advice is: trust your gut. Again, you're the parent of your kids, and you know them best. We'd say between six weeks and two months would be about right, but that's us, and our kids. Yours might be different.

If you are planning on introducing your kids to your new lady friend or gentleman caller, you might like to give your ex a heads-up for the sake of decency, but we can't really see the point of it if you've been separated for quite some time (say, over eighteen months)—unless the point is you're making a point, and then by all means, go for it.

Rebekah and her new partner managed to (generally) successfully create a blended family of five kids. They both took it very slowly and did not introduce each other to their children for more than two months. Then they very slowly introduced all of the children to each other over another six months or so. The feedback from the children has been that this made them feel like they were important and cared for. They didn't feel like their needs and wishes were ignored, so as a result, the family unit is very close and very strong, even with the children moving into the teenage years.

Letting go

The question of when to introduce new partners brings us to another concept: letting go. One of the hardest things to do in a divorce is to let go and accept that, to a very large degree, you can't legally control what your former spouse does.

The things that drove you crazy when you were married will still drive you crazy. The way they never put the kids to bed, and let them roam around the house all night? That will still happen. The way they don't seem to ever realise that kids need three meals and two snacks a day? They still won't. How they think it's okay to lie in bed until 10 a.m. on a Sunday while your six- and four-year-olds free range? They'll still do that.

With the exception of very serious issues, such as actual abuse, alcoholism and drug use, divorce means that you don't really have much of a say in your ex's parenting anymore. This is a truly great thing in some cases, but can be very difficult to get used to.

Unless you're excited by the prospect of trying to remotely control your ex-spouse when they have the kids, letting go is a really big and important step in separating. One way you can start to let go is by demonstrating to your kids that, apart from a high-level rundown of what they got up to during their time with their other parent, you're not going to grill them on the minutiae. What you don't know won't upset you. You don't want to know they ate grilled cheese sandwiches at every meal every day and spent the whole day having awesome fun at the beach rather than doing some maths homework.

Letting go is hard. Things will annoy you. This is normal. Over time, you will learn not to fire off a nasty text to your ex when you hear something they've said or done with the kids, but rather you will simply move on with your day or night. There's a reason you're divorcing them and that's because they are super annoying and selfish (probably).

The following list comprises things that clients have raised with Rebekah over the years, and they are all annoying:

- Your kids might smell different when they come home. (This is a weird one but something that loads of parents comment on. Different houses smell different and we generally don't notice it until it's our own kids who smell funny. We think it has something to do with different laundry powders, too.)

- Your ex may try on the Disneyland-parent phenomena, whereby the time with the other parent is an action-packed adventure, with presents and shopping and dinners out, from start to finish. Your ex may in fact actually take your kids to Disneyland. Some take their kids to every Disneyland in existence on all four continents. Or they take their kids heli-skiing on glaciers (this, apparently, is indeed a thing). It's upsetting but there's nothing you can do about it. You can ask a few questions about their trip and then leave it at that—there's no need to torture yourself with the details.

- Your kids may arrive home hungry, with unwashed, nit-infested hair, muddy clothes, and exhausted from two sleepovers in a row, and the ensuing meltdowns are all your problem.

- Alternatively, they will come home to you raving about how they had the *most* amazing time at the *most* amazing places, and you will be gutted. You will feel like the mean old grouch who shrieks endlessly, 'Put on your shoes!' or 'Where is your hat!?' while the other parent is clearly the SuperFunParent™. These events will all be scrupulously recorded on Facebook and Insta by your ex (or even worse, your ex's new partner) and your children, if they're old enough, will be tagged in a million pictures in amazing locations for you to look at while you're sitting at home alone. But kids know who makes their lunches and comes to their concerts and goes to parent–teacher interviews. One magical holiday doesn't cancel out fifty-two Saturday sport sessions.

- You may feel excluded from school functions or the kids' events. Don't allow this to happen. Claim your place in the institutions in your children's lives. As far as is humanly possible, always go to school functions, such as daddy and daughter dances, Father's Day breakfasts, Mother's Day afternoon teas, end-of-year concerts and daycare Christmas parties. Don't take your new partner unless your split is very amicable—this is about your kid, nobody else. If you don't seem to be able to find out when things are on, ring the school or daycare office and ask how the information is sent out. Usually there's an app or a weekly email with a newsletter—you must read it every week and take note of important events. At the same time, if your ex never turns up to things and then whines to you that they didn't know about it, tell them to talk to the school or sporting club. You're not their secretary.

- The kids' uniforms may arrive in a plastic bag, filthy dirty, and you'll be expected to wash and dry them in time for school. (This one is very annoying and Not. On. At. All. Get it put in your orders or plan that uniforms must be washed before the kids arrive. You're not the domestic help.)
- The kids will be dropped home either twelve minutes early or nine minutes late every single time. Usually, this wouldn't matter but when it's your ex doing it every second week, or every week, it is annoying as all get out. One way to mitigate this is to get your kids a smartphone, and download 'Find My Friends' or a similar app. It means you can keep an eye on how far away they are and not be caught out or worried.
- Your ex may limit the kids' ability to contact you, no matter what your plan or orders say. Or, your ex might call the kids every single night just as you sit down to dinner. It's important that children have regular contact with both parents—but it has to be at a convenient time, and it can't be intrusive. Long, daily FaceTime calls can be intrusive—your ex shouldn't get a daily look into your life, and it can really make it hard for you to move on and feel comfortable in your own home. Ordering

the children to show you around the other parent's house while you are FaceTiming or Skyping them is also not okay. The key here is compromise and communication—agree to a quick, no more than ten-minute FaceTime or phone call each night around 7.30, and stick to it.

- Your ex may think that parenting is palming the kids off onto grandparents. This is annoying, especially if you don't get many opportunities to go out yourself. But as long as your former mother- and/or father-in-law loves the kids and looks after them well, don't worry about it. It's really good for the kids to have secure grandparent relationships.
- If there's a significant money differential between the two homes, it will break your heart when you see photos of the kids dressed up in fancy clothes from Seed or Country Road that you couldn't possibly afford, and that they're 'not allowed' to bring back to your place. You'll put them in their $4 t-shirts from Kmart and you'll feel bad, even though you know perfectly well that they're all made in the same factory anyway.
- Your ex might move an inconvenient distance away (say, thirty minutes' drive) and then insist that you organise all the children's after-school activities on your days, which means that you basically end up trying to squish in dance, drama, sports training, doctor and dentist appointments into three or four days a week, even if they only have the kids every second week. When there's more than one kid, and more than one kid's worth of activities, this gets even harder, especially as the kids get older.
- Your ex might make some grand gesture like buying a house with a pool and a waterslide or getting a puppy—or two puppies! Three puppies! Three puppies and a kitten and a llama! Try as hard as you can not to fall into the trap of parenting as a spectator sport. Parenting is something you *do*,

not something you *win*. If there's one thing kids are great at, it's spotting a phony. They know who's a loving and consistent parent, and they know when they're being bought off.

- Alternatively, your ex might live in a share house and spend all their time smoking bongs, refusing to get a job, or pay child support, or in any way look after your children, while you work two jobs and raise your kids single-handed without a cent from your ex or even a night off.

- Your ex may assume that you have no life at all, you sad loser, and that you will still be at their beck and call for babysitting duties even during their time with the kids. If you were treated as the live-in nanny during your marriage, you can bet this will get worse once you've split. We know one man who actually refers to his ex-wife as his paid nanny, and treats her as such. This guy is a jerk—don't be this guy, and don't let your ex treat you like you're the help. You have your own life and you're entitled to live it.

- If you repartner, you may find that your kids and/or your ex suddenly have a serious drama (like broken bones that turn out to actually not be broken at all when you've rushed over) … every … single … time you go out for dinner with the new love of your life.

- Another common scenario is The Case of the Disappearing Parent. This is where, of course, a parent opts out of their kids' lives for huge chunks of time, or in total. A funny (and not funny ha-ha) truth is that while the courts can force a parent to make their kids spend time with their other parent, they can't (won't) force a parent to spend time with their kids. This is *very* distressing, for the parent left literally holding the baby, and the kids. A good counsellor, including one from the kids' school, can help the children come to terms with this horrible situation.

- Your ex may be completely uninterested and uninvolved in the kids' schooling, leaving every bit of the thought-load on you, with the ensuing millions of excursions and notes and forms to fill in all on your shoulders.
- Alternatively, after years of disdainful non-interest, your ex may suddenly become parent of the year once they've repartnered, and be at every school function and get voted onto the parents' association and give speeches at every single assembly.
- Your ex might insist that their new partner accompany them at all times, including on every pick up and drop off. You'll feel scrutinised in your own house, it can make changeovers incredibly stressful, and it's pretty uncomfortable all round. This is especially common when the ex has left the marriage for their affair partner.
- Things will get left at one house or another—things that the kids need, like musical instruments, swimming costumes, maths books and iPhone chargers. As far as humanly possible, have duplicates of everything at both homes. When it's important homework that's been left behind, the parent whose house it was left at should return it.
- There will be disputes over whether the kids can take their clothes and belongings from one house to another and back again. This is a really touchy issue, particularly as kids get older. We've heard of one case where the kids were forced to strip naked in the hall on changeovers, so the dad could take 'his' clothes back to his house. Don't do this. It's incredibly upsetting and it damages your children. As annoying as it is to not have clothes returned, try to remember that your ex isn't wearing your daughter's underpants and new jacket. They are your kids' clothes, not yours. Let them wear them where they want. The same goes for birthday and Christmas presents.

They're not presents for 'your' house—they are presents for your children.

- Some people expect their exes to pack the kids a bag and unpack it at the end, meaning they're the only one who ever does any washing. This isn't on. Your ex must have enough things like clothes, toothbrushes and the like at their own house for their children.
- Your ex might engage in really sneaky surveillance of you, and constantly imply that you're an unfit parent and that you're putting the kids in danger by doing totally normal things like taking them to the beach or the pool. Or you might find yourself stalking your ex while they have the kids, under the cover of 'keeping an eye on them'.

All these things, and more, will annoy you. They annoy all separated parents universally. But unless you fancy living your life in constant conflict with your ex, you must learn to let it go. These are generally not matters (with the exception of the last one, which can become problematic) that you want to be involved in litigation over for years to come.

It is very easy to get yourself completely worked up, and it's very hard to let go of control when it comes to your children. But that's what divorce is—not worrying about or being overly invested in what your ex does. You're not divorced *to* them, you're divorced *from* them.

Case study—Amy and Nidhish

Amy and Nidhish were together for nine years. They had two children, Katia and Erina, aged three and four. The split was relatively amicable, and the girls lived one week with Amy, and one week with Nidhish.

Things got complicated when Nidhish moved into an apartment complex with a pool. Amy had always been very anxious about the girls around water, following a very scary near drowning she suffered as a child. Because of this the girls had attended swimming lessons from babyhood, and were water aware, at least to an age-appropriate level.

Amy tried to insist that Nidhish would promise not to take the girls swimming during his time with them. She was extremely upset about the prospect of Nidhish supervising two young children without her there.

In the beginning, Nidhish agreed to Amy's demands. Over the course of the summer, however, he started to resent what he felt was Amy's unreasonable attempt to control him. Amy refused to pay attention to Nidhish's attempts to show Amy that he would carefully supervise the girls. In time, it became a major source of tension and Nidhish decided that he would take the girls swimming one hot Saturday afternoon. When he dropped the girls back to Amy, they immediately told her they had spent the afternoon in the pool.

Amy, furious and crying, rang her lawyer the following Monday to demand that they seek orders from the Family Court banning Nidhish from taking the children swimming. Her lawyer said that such an order was extremely unlikely to ever be made, and recommended instead that Amy seek counselling to help her deal with her anxieties over the girls being taken swimming while in Nidhish's care.

The lesson here is that as long as your kids are safe with their other parent (and if you're a very vigilant Type A parent, you may need to practise letting go even more) and reasonably well looked after, let the small stuff go as much as possible. Repeat to yourself, 'Not my circus, not my monkeys'. Be the Sane Parent.

Pick your battles. After all, you'll need your strength for …

Dealing with the Department of Human Services, and other adventures in bureaucratic nightmares

You've probably already had dealings with the Department of Human Services (DHS—or whatever their name is this week. And frankly, whoever thought up the current incarnation ought to take a good hard look at themselves; it sounds like the name of a processing plant for human cadavers). DHS is the government department responsible for Centrelink, the child support agency, and family payments, among much else. You've no doubt registered for your myGov account and promptly lost the 27-digit password, and had to answer secret questions you can't even remember hearing before, let alone supplying an answer to, such as 'What was the name of your first grade teacher?' (Hint: the answer must be written exactly as it was originally, so if you wrote Mrs. Winters the first time, you can't subsequently write Mrs Winters or mrs Winters or Mrs winters or mrswinters or mrs winters or Ms Winters. And invariably you'll get locked out of the system while trying to remember precisely how you wrote it the first time.)

You will therefore know what a complete and utter nightmare of a bureaucratic disaster each and every dealing with them is and will be forever more. So just accept that every man, woman and child in Australia hates dealing with DHS, and let's get on with it.

One handy tool on the DHS website is the child support estimator.[42] Without needing an account (yay), you can punch in your details, the amount of children you have, how many nights of care you have a week/fortnight/month, and your income, plus your ex's income, and you'll get a fairly accurate idea of the level of child support you'll either receive or have to pay.

Depending on your circumstances you'll be shocked or appalled at how little it seems to be. For many families, the amount will barely even cover the cost of child care. This is a really awful part of divorce. It's important to note that the child support estimate is the *minimum* that a paying parent must pay, not the *maximum*. Many families reach their own agreements over paying for things over and

42 processing.csa.gov.au/estimator/About.aspx.

above the estimate, such as contributing to child care or after school care, school fees, orthodontics, big ticket items such as laptops for school, and so on. Each family is different, and most paying parents are very keen to ensure their kids don't go without. We'll talk more about this in Chapter 7.

It's often a good idea to take the day off work and go into Centrelink (if you can find one) and talk through all the various payments or subsidies you might be entitled to now that you're single. There's quite a few, and they change all the time, so it's best to talk it through with an officer at Centrelink if you can, but the government seems to want to make that as difficult as possible (probably because they don't want to employ people to provide advice to their actual customers).

In the absence of a real person to talk to, a good place to start is the DHS website (www.humanservices.gov.au) and then go to the Payment and Service Finder page, which will prompt you to provide information so that it can match you to payments or concessions you might be eligible for. You'll also have to update your family income assessment, and notify them that you've separated, which can also be done 'easily' online. (Haha! Hahaha!)

Which brings us nicely to the next chapter—your parenting negotiations. You might want to get a cup of tea first—or a big glass of something stronger.

WORKSHEET 4
QUESTIONS FOR MY LAWYER AT OUR FIRST CONFERENCE

This worksheet is so you can jot down any questions you have for your lawyer before you go into the meeting or teleconference.

Remembering that lawyers charge up to $600 an hour in six-minute units, it's very important that you don't waste your money by not having a really clear idea of what questions you want answered.

Date:	**Date:**
Questions for my lawyer at our first conference	**Answers**
1.	
2.	
3.	
4.	
5.	
6.	
7.	
8.	
9.	
10.	

6
Your parenting negotiations

The family law system as it relates to your parenting arrangements can be a frightening and confusing place. It's a world of strange jargon and at stake are the most important people in the world to you—your children—and those stakes are the highest they'll ever be.

We've talked in Chapter 5 about having a game plan for what your best negotiated outcome would be, and what your worst negotiated outcome would be. This chapter provides more information on the choices you're going to have to make—and be warned, there's a lot to it. If stuff in this chapter doesn't apply to you, feel free to skip ahead, because some of it is heavy going.

And remember: its family *law*, not family *war*. You will be co-parenting with your ex for years to come. Don't let yourself get into a position where things become completely toxic if you can possibly help it. Some things aren't forgivable—and persecuting your ex over your children to the fullest extent of the law is one of those things. Unless you plan on having separate birthdays and weddings for your children, and separate christenings and the like for your grandchildren, tread carefully, no matter how angry you are. All you can hope is that your ex will extend you the same courtesy. Be the Sane Parent.

'Lives with' and 'spends time with' and other lawyer gobbledegook

First up, let's get the basic terminology right.

In Australia, 'custody' is now referred to as who the child 'lives with', access or contact is who the child 'spends time with' and 'guardianship' is now 'parental responsibility'. These terms are different again in state child protection courts. The change of terminology in the Family Law Act was to get away from the idea that one parent controlled a child and permitted the other parent to see them. Kids aren't possessions, after all, so it is helpful to have terminology that doesn't treat them like they are objects to be passed around.

If children are spending relatively long periods of time with both parents, then it is usual to have orders saying that they live with both parents. Even if the periods with both parents are not completely equal, it may be a comfort for the children to know that they live with both parents, rather than live with one parent and visit the other.

It is extremely important that child-focused language is used when you are discussing your children. You must refer to the children as 'our children' not 'my children' where possible. For example, say 'I want the best outcome for our children, which is why I believe XYZ'. Using language that includes your children's other parent is very important, and the courts have made adverse comments about parents who use language that demonstrates that they see the children as 'theirs' and theirs alone.

Self-representing in the family law system

Many people choose to represent themselves in the family law system. Figures suggest that in more than half of all cases, either one or both parties are self-represented. It's easy to understand why—many people don't quite qualify for Legal Aid and the cost of lawyers is, sadly, prohibitive for many. This is very unfair and upsetting.

Lawyers like to say that anyone who represents themselves has a fool for a client. This isn't true. There's a huge amount of information available online about running your own family law matter, especially if it's relatively simple and straightforward, but you must take care not to fall into a rabbit warren of internet crazies pushing an agenda.

There's also the option of not wholly self-representing, but asking your lawyer to allow you to do as much as possible of the grunt work on your matter to keep costs down. This can be a really good halfway position.

Most lawyers are semi-decent people who don't particularly want to stiff single parents, and if yours won't at least discuss with you how you can work together to reduce costs as much as possible, get a new lawyer.

What sorts of orders can the courts make in relation to children?

Before we get too far into this chapter, let's take a brief look at the types of orders the courts can make in relation to children, following the separation of their parents.

First up, as we've already discussed, the court can make orders relating to who the child lives with, and who the child spends time with. These orders can also include grandparents or other significant people in a child's life.

Case study—Alethia

Alethia was the grandmother of Charlie. Charlie's parents were George and Anna. Alethia was George's mother.

For four years, since Charlie was six months old, Alethia looked after him two days a week. When George and Anna separated, Anna decided that she didn't want Alethia to care for Charlie anymore. Although it took many months, the Federal Circuit Court eventually ordered that Charlie spend two afternoons per week with Alethia, with Alethia picking Charlie up from school and dropping him back to Anna's home by 6 p.m.

The courts can also make orders relating to:

- who the child communicates with and when/how the child communicates with that person
- parental responsibility (which we'll discuss later on)
- granting sole parental responsibility over certain issues (such as medical decisions, which we'll talk more about later on)
- injunctions (which is where the court orders a party to stop doing something, such as using a different name for a child, which, again, we'll go into more detail about in this chapter)
- authorising schools, daycare centres, extracurricular activity providers and medical professionals to provide information and documents to each parent
- compulsory mediation between parents if a dispute arises about the orders (unless a matter is urgent)
- child maintenance for a child who is not covered by the DHS.

It's worth pointing out that the family law courts are horribly underfunded, and that this leads to delays and frustrations with the system.

If you can sort out your issues with your ex without having to go to court, you will all be better off for it both mentally and financially. The family law courts should be for only the most complex, difficult matters, and generally they are.

The best interests of the children

When you're in the family law system, you will hear the phrase 'in the best interests of the children' over and over again. Legally, it's the paramount consideration of the judge, as mandated by the *Family Law Act 1975*.

But what does 'the best interests of the children' mean?

It means that the family law system must ensure that any decision the judge makes is in the best interests of the children. We've put this up the front of the chapter because it's the most important aspect of understanding how decisions are made if your matter goes to court, but also to show you the principles that you should keep in mind before it gets to that point, so you can hopefully avoid it.

The Family Law Act sets out factors that the judge must take into account when considering whether to make an order or not, and those factors include the following primary considerations:

Primary considerations	
The benefit to the child of having a meaningful relationship with both of the child's parents.	Sometimes, very, very rarely, a court will find that there simply is no benefit to the child of having a relationship with a parent. This is very uncommon and usually follows abuse or neglect or a finding of 'unacceptable risk' of abuse, neglect or exposure to family violence. Usually the court will find there is a benefit to the child of having a meaningful relationship with both parents, and will look at whether the arrangements will make the relationships meaningful into the future.
The need to protect the child from physical or psychological harm from being subjected to, or exposed to, abuse, neglect or family violence.	This consideration is now given more weight than whether the relationship will be meaningful. A child has the right to be safe and a court may need evidence from criminal histories, or clinical notes from a doctor or hospital, a family report writer or psychiatrist on this point. If you hold a fear that a child is not safe, then you must seek urgent legal advice.
Secondary considerations	
Any views of the child/ren.	This is stuff like how old the children are, how emphatic their views are and how much they understand what those views mean to them. Just be careful with this one; children usually love both parents and will usually tell both parents that they want to live with them—kids generally want to live with both parents all the time and want both parents to just get on with it and stop bothering them with stupid questions.
Nature of the child's relationship with both parents, with their grandparents, their siblings, step-siblings etc.	As much as you may hate this, your children probably love both parents and their grandparents (and their siblings—whatever form their siblings take: step-siblings, half-siblings. Kids choose their family based on who they love, not necessarily who's biologically related to them).

The extent to which each parent has taken the opportunity to actually parent.	This can be a tricky one. If during the relationship it was convenient for one parent to work all the time and one parent to do the parenting, it can be very upsetting to find that the previously absent parent is suddenly trying to be the parent of the year, especially when you have always done the hard work like the school run, the interminable meetings and appointments with the doctors/teachers/coaches/speech therapists. It is natural to be suspicious of the sudden reversal. Equally, it can be upsetting to suddenly find that your kids are growing up and you hardly know them—this tends to put the importance of that job you actually hate into perspective. Separation, no matter who initiated it, generally comes with a huge re-evaluation of priorities.
The extent to which the parents have actually paid for the kids.	Let's be honest, kids are expensive little things and a court is unlikely to be massively sympathetic to someone who will not pay child support.
The likely effect of change on the child.	This counts especially if there is going to be a separation from parents, siblings, step-siblings, grandparents. For example, the likely effect of the proposed arrangements on a child could be that the child is going to go from living primarily with Mum to living with both parents. Or it could be that the child is going to go from living with both parents in Adelaide to living with Dad in Sydney. What effect will this have on the child and how will you both work to minimise the effect on the child?
The practical difficulties and expense with respect to the children seeing and communicating with both parents and whether that difficulty or expense will substantially affect the child's right to maintain personal relations and direct contact with both parents on a regular basis.	This factor is most relevant when a relocation away from a parent is being proposed. Australians are mobile and our land is vast. Cases where a parent proposes to move to Brisbane from Sydney, or to Perth from Canberra are very common. Even if the move is by consent, the registrar will want to see in your application for consent orders form how you have agreed to make sure the kids still see and communicate with their other parents and extended family.

The capacity of both parents to provide for the needs of the child, including emotional and intellectual needs.	Sometimes a parent simply does not have the capacity to parent, whether because of an intellectual disability or because they are in jail or affected by drugs and alcohol, and this can be tragic. It is something the court needs to know about.
The maturity, sex, lifestyle and background of the child and the child's parents and any characteristics of the child that the court thinks is relevant.	It is important that a child be able to fully participate in their life, including in their sports, their activities such as dance and drama, their culture and their religion, and that they are able to hang out with their friends. A court is unlikely to be sympathetic to someone who says that they want shared care but is unwilling to take the child to their dance recital if the child loves to dance. And, thankfully, long gone are the days where a mother repartnering with another woman was something the court had to worry about (check out the decision of the court in 'In the Marriage of L',* and the unbelievable eight questions that the court thought were appropriate to ask—such as 'whether a homosexual parent would show the same love and responsibility as a heterosexual parent').
If the child is an Aboriginal or Torres Strait Islander child, then the court must consider how the arrangements will make sure the child's right to enjoy that culture with other people who share that culture is protected.	For Aboriginal and Torres Strait Islander children, maintaining their cultural ties is an important consideration.
The attitude to the child, and to the responsibilities of parenthood, demonstrated by each of the child's parents.	Generally both parents have been good, attentive parents to the best of their abilities, given the roles taken on during the relationship. Occasionally a parent will not have been so into parenting and it can be tempting to consider that a sudden interest in being the parent of the year has been spurred by a DHS assessment or by you repartnering. This may well be the case, but it does not necessarily mean that the sudden interest is not genuine, or more importantly, in your child's best interest. On the other hand, a parent who has a history of making very bad choices will have to work pretty hard to convince a court that they will start meeting the responsibilities of parenthood. Regularly returning dirty urinalysis results is unlikely to convince a judge that you can do it.

Any family violence and family violence orders made.	This is important, as if there has been family violence and/or a family violence order made and depending on the circumstances around the order being made, then the court has to consider how the proposed arrangements fit in with the primary consideration of any need to protect the child.
Whether it would be preferable to make the order that would be least likely to lead to the institution of further proceedings in relation to the child.	This is also known as 'if we make these orders, are we all going to be back in court again next month?'
Any other factors the court can think of.	It's really quite involved. But the idea behind the Family Law Act is to, as far as possible, ensure: 'that children receive adequate and proper parenting to help them achieve their full potential, and to ensure that parents fulfil their duties, and meet their responsibilities, concerning the care, welfare and development of their children'.**

* 'In the Marriage of L' (1983) FLC 91-353 www.austlii.edu.au/cgi-bin/viewdoc/au/cases/cth/FamCA/1983/20.html.

** *The Family Law Act 1975*.

In non-lawyer talk, this means that children must have every opportunity to be cared for by both parents, if this is in the children's best interests. In Australian family law, there is the presumption that parents will have equal shared **parental responsibility** for their children,[43] but this does not mean there's a presumption that parents will 'get' equal time.

> **Parental responsibility**—in relation to a child, means all the duties, powers, responsibilities and authority that, by law, parents have in relation to children.[44]

Notice how that definition does not mention 'rights' at all? In family law matters, parents do not have rights, children have rights.

Shared parental responsibility means that parents jointly make decisions about **major long-term issues** regarding the children.

42 Section 61DA *Family Law Act 1975*.

44 Section 61B *Family Law Act 1975*.

Major long-term issues—issues of the care, welfare and development of a child of a long-term nature include (but are not limited to):

- the child's education (both current and future)
- the child's religious and cultural upbringing
- the child's health
- the child's name
- changes to the child's living arrangements that make it significantly more difficult for the child to spend time with a parent.

For example, a parent's decision to enter a relationship with a new partner and for their child to form a relationship with the new partner is not, of itself, a major long-term issue in relation to the child. However, the decision will involve a major long-term issue if, for example, the relationship with the new partner involves the parent moving to another area and the move will make it significantly more difficult for the child to spend time with the other parent.[45]

It also doesn't mean that the kids will necessarily live 50 per cent of the time with Dad, and 50 per cent of the time with Mum (this is known as 'shared care' or 'equal parenting time'). In the event of a dispute over that, which can't be resolved by the parents alone, the court will consider the best interests of the children, *and* the practicality of any orders, before making a decision. The High Court in MRR v. GR ruled that the family law courts have to consider the practicality of shared care. It's not the case that the court will order that Mum must live in a caravan park in a remote mining town where she's unable to get a job because she and Dad moved there before they split, and Dad now wants shared care. [46]

What is a parenting plan?

A parenting plan is a document that records an agreement between parents relating to the care of and arrangements for their children post-separation.

45 Section 4, *Family Law Act 1975*.

46 MRR v. GR [2010] HCA 4, http://eresources.hcourt.gov.au/showCase/2010/HCA/4.

They are generally drafted by parents together, sometimes with the help of a lawyer or a mediator, and are best suited to quite amicable separations where the parents can still work together for the benefit of the kids. As we mentioned earlier in this chapter, in family law, we don't talk about 'custody' anymore, but, rather, we talk about 'contact' between parents.

A parenting plan can include such things as:

- Who the children will live with, and when they will spend time with each of their parents (contact hours).
- Who will drop the children off to school and who will pick them up.
- An undertaking that school uniforms must be washed and lunchboxes emptied during contact weekends.
- Where the children will spend special days such as Christmas and birthdays, including the times that they will be dropped off and picked up and by whom (and see Chapter 8 for more information on holidays).
- Whether a parent will be given the opportunity to look after the children if the other parent can't during their allotted time—this is known as the first right of refusal to care, and generally relates to overnight absences by a parent, and can get tricky if a step-parent is routinely caring for a child in place of a parent.
- How decisions to enrol the children in extracurricular activities (such as maths tutoring, ballet classes or weekend sports) will be made.
- How major decisions relating to health, education, religion and their last names will be made between the parents. (Note: decisions such as when to give a child cough syrup do not constitute a medical decision. This is a parenting decision that should be made by the parent who is caring for the child—see more on medical disputes further on.)

- How decisions on body-altering procedures such as tattoos or body piercing (including ear-piercing) will be made.
- Where the children will live, and the circumstances in which they can move.
- How finances will be handled, including:
  - who pays for birthday presents for the children's friends
  - who pays pocket money
  - who pays for the teacher's end-of-year present
  - who pays the tooth fairy, and when do you stop
  - who pays the school fees
  - who pays for school excursions, camps and uniforms
  - who pays for the children's birthday parties, and whether they will be held jointly with both parents present or separately with one parent on a year-about schedule
  - who pays for tutoring and music lessons and dance classes
  - who pays for the tech—the iPhones, the iPads, the compulsory school laptop
  - who pays when the iPhone is dropped down the toilet or smashed, or the laptop is broken or left on a sports field, or the power cord is left on the train
  - who pays for pharmacy products, such as nit treatments (endless, endless nit treatments)
  - who pays for sports equipment like basketball boots, mouthguards, dance costumes and tennis racquets
  - who pays for the formal dresses and tux hire, corsages and entry tickets to school formals and dinners

- who pays for the dentist, orthodontist and other specialists, and the gap for the doctor
- who pays for lunch orders
- who pays child support payments and how much.

- When the parents can ring or FaceTime the children and how long for, and on what specific number the child can be contacted on (disputes over whether calls can be made to mobile telephones or to home landlines are not unheard of).
- What happens if one or both of the parents die.
- How changeovers will be handled (see later in this chapter for more on changeovers).
- Where changeovers will occur.
- The role of grandparents and other significant people in the lives of the children, from 'both sides' of the family.
- And a range of other matters, including when the plan will be renegotiated as the children grow and their needs change.

As you'll appreciate, there is an enormous amount of information needed for an ironclad parenting plan that picks up on all the issues that can arise in raising kids. It's almost impossible to cover everything, but you can make life easier by working through the list above. It won't always work—we know one bloke who won't pay for his kid's nit treatments because it's 'not a pharmaceutical product but a therapeutic product'.

Relationships Australia has an excellent online resource that allows parents to draft a parenting plan together without the need for lawyers. You can find it at: www.relationships.org.au/relationship-advice/publications/pdfs/share-the-care-parenting-plan.

What are consent orders?

Consent orders are legally binding orders made by the Family Court or Federal Circuit Court. They are arrangements relating to your children that you and your ex have agreed to, just like a parenting plan (and include the same considerations as in the list above), but they have the added protections of being legally binding (in other words, they are enforceable by the Family Court or the Federal Circuit Court).

Of course, they will generally be drafted by a lawyer, and are much more expensive than a parenting plan, but they are brilliant if you think your ex won't comply with a parenting plan (or has shown that they won't).

Both parties must get independent legal advice (this means advice given to you by a solicitor who hasn't also advised your ex) before signing the orders. Relatively simple orders drafted by a lawyer will cost about $5000.

If you breach the orders without a reason, your ex can seek a '**contravention** order', which can have very serious penalties, particularly if you're a repeat offender. You can be ordered to pay a fine, pay your ex's legal costs, attend parenting programs, or even, in very serious cases, go to prison.

> **Contravention**— when a court finds a party has not followed a court order (including consent orders), that party is in contravention of (broken the terms of) the order. There are penalties that apply to contraventions of a court order, which can range from a fine to, possibly, imprisonment.

The court can also find that a parent had a **reasonable excuse** for breaching the orders.

> **Reasonable excuse**—a judge *may* find that someone has a reasonable excuse for breaching parenting orders if the person did not understand them, or the person breached the orders because it was necessary to protect the health or safety of a person (whether that person was the person breaching the orders or the child, or someone else entirely). The key word here is 'reasonable', and what might feel reasonable in the middle of a heated argument may not feel so reasonable in the cold hard light of a courtroom when confronted by an

angry judge. Get legal advice before taking matters into your own hands.

Which one do I need—parenting plan or consent orders?

If there's been infidelity, violence or any kind of abusive behaviour between the parents, it can be much harder to negotiate a parenting plan together. Parenting plans are best suited to situations where the parents are still reasonably amicable, and can discuss things like what happens when one of you gets a new partner, without wanting to set fire to one another's belongings.

If you're not very amicable and are still in the anger stage of grief, or either parent has shown a great reluctance to follow through with the agreements reached in the plan, consent orders are a good option. They can actually work to reduce conflict by having a very clear, legally binding set of rules that each parent must follow (within reason).

Consent orders are as binding on both parties as if the court had made them itself after a full trial. As we have discussed, they must be complied with, and not just passively complied with. You have to positively comply and that might mean taking steps to encourage children to spend time with their other parent, unless there are serious problems. If there are serious problems, you need to get further legal advice (and we'll talk more about this later). Don't forget, behaviour that might seem reasonable in the heat of an argument with your ex may not seem so reasonable in the cold hard light of day when trying to explain yourself to a judge.

You can also combine your parenting arrangements and your financial arrangements on the one application for consent orders. It is helpful if the actual consent orders that go with the application for consent orders are separated into property and parenting, as usually you need to give a copy of parenting orders to the children's school/s and doctor/s—they do not necessarily need to know the nitty-gritty of your financial arrangement and you probably don't want them to know how much your house, your car and your furniture are worth.

What if we don't have a parenting plan or consent orders?

If you don't have either a parenting plan or consent orders, you're relying on mutual good will. For some families, this can work very well. If you and your ex are great mates, live next door to one another and communicate really effectively, then there's probably no need for a written document outlining how you will co-parent. However, be aware that sometimes even the most amicable of co-parenting relationships can quickly fall apart. A new partner, a perceived slight, or the realisation that the arrangements aren't really all that fair can lead to big problems.

We're often asked questions like what happens if your ex just picks the kids up from daycare and never returns them, and all you've got is a loose arrangement with no specified time for each parent. This is the bit where family lawyers make all their money, because in cases like this you generally end up urgently going to court to get your kids back or even to spend time with them.

The best approach, in our experience, is to have a clearly documented parenting plan if you're very amicable (and have had a 'good' separation where you have mutually decided it's time to move on), and consent orders if you're not. If you think there's any chance that your ex will do something like refuse to let you see the kids for extended periods of time, then you need consent orders, because they're legally enforceable.

The state police cannot recover children unless asked to by the Federal Circuit Court or the family law courts. The state police can go and do a 'welfare check' and some officers are very good at talking sense into parents.

What are the different types of parenting arrangements?

There are as many different types of parenting arrangements as there are separated parents.

The worst kind of plans, in our experience, are ones where the kids spend time with Dad every weekend and live with Mum through the week. This means that Mum gets to do all the yelling about homework and socks while Dad gets to take them for milkshakes and brunch and to the beach.

Don't agree to this arrangement if you're the mum and don't try to insist on it if you're the dad, even if you're so busy as work that you can't spend time with your kids through the week but still want to see them on the weekend. It's just not fair to expect the other parent to do all of the heavy lifting while you get to do the super-fun, happy-time stuff.

The website *Emery on Divorce* has some brilliant examples of different parenting arrangements, broken down into age groups of the children, and including different plans for different 'styles' of divorce—for example, the 'angry' divorce, the 'distant' divorce, and the 'cooperative divorce'.[47] The type of divorce you have, and the ages of your children, will be very important considerations when it comes to working out your parenting plan.

Otherwise, the arrangements that Rebekah helps develop in her practice, which you can consider as a starting point, are given in the following table.[48]

What is the arrangement called?	How does it work in practice?	In what situations is it suitable?
Live with parent 1 (usually but not always Mum), spend time with parent 2 (usually, but not always) Dad.	The children live with Mum, and spend time with Dad every second weekend from Friday afternoon until Monday morning, and also spend time with Dad for dinner or overnight each Wednesday night, and spend equal time with both parents during school holidays.	This arrangement used to be the 'norm' and is still very common today.

47 www.emeryondivorce.com/parenting_plans.php.

48 Legal offices are called 'practices' and lawyers don't work in law, they 'practise' it. This is because nobody can ever perfect law, we're all just still learning, and it's not a science, there are no absolutes. Not very comforting, is it?

What is the arrangement called?	How does it work in practice?	In what situations is it suitable?
Equal time with a weekly changeover.	The children live with Mum and Dad equally on a time-about schedule. This means that the kids spend Sunday night to Friday morning with Mum one week, and from Friday morning till Sunday night with Dad the next week.	This arrangement is probably the most common 'equal time' plan.
Week about with an overnight.	The kids live with Mum one week, and live with dad the following week, but spend one overnight midweek with the parent whom they are not living with that week.	Suitable for angry or distant divorces where equal times have been insisted upon by one or both parents, but can also work well for cooperative divorces.
2:2:3 rotation.	The kids live with Mum for two nights, and then with Dad two nights, and then have a long weekend with Mum (three nights). The following week, the kids live with Dad for two nights, then with Mum for two nights, and then have a long weekend with Dad (three nights).	This can be a complicated arrangement and is generally only suitable for very amicable divorces where the ex spouses can work well together (because the children are always leaving stuff at the other house). There are other iterations of this plan, such as the 4:4:3, or the 3:3:4 rotations. These seem complicated but can work really well around the kids' activities, and children generally like it because they don't spend too much time away from either parent, from half-siblings or step-siblings or from pets.
Bird nesting.	The kids stay in the family home, and the parents move back and forth during their time with the children between the family home and a second residence, which may or may not be shared by the other parent.	Generally bird nesting is seen as a short-term strategy. It has the benefits of stability for the children but doesn't allow much privacy for the parents and can get complicated if a new partner is on the scene. Parents must be very amicable.

What is the arrangement called?	How does it work in practice?	In what situations is it suitable?
Come and go.	Where the children can come and go between their parents' homes as they choose.	Typically the parents will live very close by, or may share a duplex/semi and the kids will be older. Parents must be very amicable.

Do I have to let my baby or toddler spend the night with my ex?

Parenting arrangements for babies and preschoolers can be the most difficult of all to negotiate. It is really important to remember that your child is not a baby forever but the other parent is the other parent forever—the way you both behave now has the potential to set up the post-separation co-parenting relationship for a very long time to come. A mother's need to have her baby with her is primal, but in order for a child to form a close bond with their father, time together with him is essential, too. Dads can often feel bereft of time with their child and may feel like they are missing out on seeing important milestones. It's a very upsetting issue for both mums and dads, and there are no easy answers. There are no hard and fast rules either—it really does depend on the circumstances of your family. The fact that it's so hard for lawyers to be definitive about this is a huge source of frustration for many parents.

Generally speaking, if your kid isn't being breastfed and they're over the age of, say, three or four, and they otherwise have a good and close relationship with your ex, then it's highly likely the court will take the view that it is in your child's best interests to have some overnight time with their other parent.

Robyn Sexton, a Federal Circuit Court judge in the family law division, wrote an excellent paper on overnight parenting arrangements for the 0–4 years age group. Her paper can be found online and it's very readable and interesting.[49] If you can, encourage your ex to read it. It talks a lot about what we've discussed earlier in this

49 www.legalaid.nsw.gov.au/__data/assets/pdf_file/0008/9737/Parenting-Arrangements-for-0-to-4-year-olds-September-2011.pdf.

book in terms of attachment theory and the critical importance of the early years (before age five) in terms of establishing close parental bonds, while at the same time protecting your child's primary attachment.

The ideal, according to Sexton, is this:[50]

- Both parents must have a secure and warm relationship with the child before separation.
- The mother is supportive of the father/child relationship, including expressing positive feelings and reassurance on handover and reunion (and vice versa).
- Routine is consistent and predictable and the child is not away from the other parent for more than a few days at a time. (This is a very important consideration. It's not a great idea for a very young child to spend lengthy periods away from their primary carer. Sexton does note that younger children often cope better for slightly longer if they have older siblings with them on visits.)
- No conflict should be displayed in front of the child or conveyed in any way to the child.
- Both parents must communicate about and monitor the child's tolerance for the separations.
- Any increasing contact should be gradual, with continuing sensitivity to the child's reactions and behaviours. (This means that it's probably best to start with an overnight visit of one night and gradually build up to a full weekend of two or three nights and then assess if the child is coping.)
- Distress at changeover needs to be managed sensitively by both parents. Transitions handled in a negative way will increase the child's stress.

50 Adapted from Federal Magistrate Robyn Sexton's 'Parenting arrangements for 0–4 year age group'.

- Parents must be able to repair a disruption (i.e. work together to fix any anxiety caused by separations or time apart from either parent) to create a secure attachment. This means that if, for example, one night the child is with their other parent and is very upset and can't settle, then the primary carer is consulted and, if necessary, the child is returned to the primary carer without any fuss or drama.

If you are like many separated parents, the above list might feel almost impossible. It is the very definition of both parents having to be the Sane Parent. If you can, aim to get as close to the list as possible. With that in mind, it's probably best if you (if you're the primary carer) facilitate overnight visits for your child with your ex once the child is about three or four, and without the court ordering you to do so, as long as the above list is adhered to.

It reflects well on you, and most importantly, if there are no real issues of risk it's good for your child to have that time with their other parent, especially without them feeling like they are betraying you—which they are not.

When you're feeling sad about this (and you probably will feel very sad) it can be helpful to remember that doing everything you can to facilitate your kids having a great relationship with their other parent makes you a fantastic mum or dad. A close, functional relationship with both parents is critically important to your child's development and giving them that time without making anyone feel bad or guilty about it is one of the best things you can do as a parent.

Case study—Skylar and Aaron

Skylar and Aaron separated when Skylar was six months pregnant. When Alice, their baby, was born, she lived with Skylar but spent time with Aaron from birth; at first three times a week, for one-hour blocks and then, as she grew older, for more frequent and longer periods of time. He also FaceTimed her every day at 6 p.m. to say goodnight, even when she was a barely sentient newborn blob.

As Alice was breastfed until eighteen months of age, Aaron didn't push for overnights.

When she turned two, Skylar asked Aaron if he would look after Alice for the night of Skylar's office Christmas party. Slowly, over the next year, Alice more frequently spent the night with Aaron, and by age three, she was spending time with him every second Friday night from after daycare until 4 p.m. Saturday. Aaron and Alice also went to Bali together for four days when Alice was four. When she turned five, she started spending every second Friday and Saturday night with Aaron, returning home at lunchtime on Sunday. When she started school, Alice started spending time from after school Friday to before school Monday every second weekend with her dad, and half of school holidays with each parent. When she started high school, Alice spent equal time with both parents.

Alice grew into a very happy little girl with strong attachments to both Skylar and Aaron.

What are the normal arrangements for tweens and teens?

When you separate and you have older children, the arrangements can be quite different from those suitable for younger children.

Once over the age of, say, ten or twelve (the court has taken a child's wishes into account from a younger age than this, but it's a good guide, and we're deliberately vague here because it really depends on the maturity of the child), the child can have fairly substantial input into the contact arrangements on their own behalf.

An older teenager, such as a fifteen- or sixteen-year-old, might elect to not have overnights at all, but instead might meet their mum or dad for dinner a few times a week, and for Sunday lunch. Or, they might spend Saturday nights with their other parent but leave quite early the next day. In circumstances where a young adult has clearly stated they do not want to spend overnights with one of their parents, it would be very unusual for a court to make any sort of order, and even more unusual still for a contravention order to be made in circumstances where a teenager has voted with their feet.

This can be very difficult for the parent who doesn't live with the teenager to cope with. It can feel like a crushing blow, and for the parent the teen does live with, the fact that they have no young-adult-free time at all can also be quite difficult. It can be pretty tough on the teenager, too; they will most likely be very worried about hurting their parent, but at the same time doesn't want to keep the same schedule as their younger siblings, or the schedule that was devised when they were much younger.

There's not much that can be done about a teenager who doesn't want to spend overnights away from their main residence anymore, except to try to carve out time with the teen, and create a new, more adult relationship. It can help to try to encourage a 'come and go' policy, where your teen feels comfortable coming to and going from your house as they please, which might encourage them to see you more if they're not being pressured to do so. You can, of course, go to court, and ask them to enforce the consent orders, but as our dad says, good luck trying to make a fifteen-year-old do anything to which they are diametrically opposed. You might as well try to stop the sun rising in the morning while you're at it.

Teenagers who have lived through highly conflictual separations generally do vote with their feet. Worse still, they can decide 'a pox on both your houses' and take themselves off to live with extended family or friends, in households where they perceive things to be 'normal'. Rebekah has seen parents who, too late, realise that the decade they spent fighting with one another resulted in a teenager simply having had enough and not wanting to be much involved with either parent anymore.

My ex wants fifty-fifty care of the children, but we can't get along at all!

There's a curious phenomenon in family law matters whereby some separated parents who are completely at war with one another think that the best way to resolve this is to have even more to do with one another by co-parenting half the time each.

Family lawyers call this the 'we cannot co-parent, therefore we must co-parent more' conundrum. It is entirely standard for one parent to threaten to take the other parent back to court to try to get fifty-fifty shared care (also known as equal parenting time) in an attempt to get their own way on some other matter.

The court will more than likely not order shared care where parents cannot even decide on the most basic matters together without conflict. This isn't to say that it never happens, just that open warfare between former spouses reduces the likelihood of equal parenting time being ordered. Shared care, or even substantial and significant time, is generally only suitable where parents are amicable and are able to work together in the best interests of their children.

If we look at the Family Law Act (and why not? It's so riveting!), we will see what the court thinks about parents at war. The Family Court's primary considerations in determining what is in the best interests of a child include: '(a) the benefit to the child of having a meaningful relationship with both of the child's parents; and (b) the need to protect the child from physical or psychological harm from being subjected to, or exposed to, abuse, neglect or family violence'.

We know that parents who are openly at war with one another are subjecting their children to psychological harm. We also know that co-parenting, especially fifty-fifty, requires a great deal of patience, understanding and cooperation, and isn't suited to angry divorces. The case law on this clearly supports the notion that shared care and joint parental time are best suited to parents who get along.

Case study—Misha and Toni

Misha and Toni separated after five years together. They had two children, James and Ava, aged seven and nine. Misha was a schoolteacher and Toni was a vet. When they split, they were very keen to remain friends, and Toni bought a two-bedroom house around the corner from the home she formerly shared with Misha.

They decided that they would share the time they spent with the children equally, with James and Ava spending four days with Misha and then four days with Toni in turn on a rolling schedule. Toni also did parent reading at the school three mornings a week, and Misha picked the children up from after-school care each day, as she worked at the same school, and dropped them to Toni when Toni finished work.

It was their intention that as the children grew older, they would be able to go between the two houses as they wished. Most Wednesday nights, all four family members met for sushi for dinner. Misha and Toni also had a parenting meeting each fortnight where they met for coffee and discussed matters relating to the children in a more structured way.

We can see from this case study that Misha and Toni have been able to share the time they spend with their children equally because they live close by one another, they both have flexible and supportive workplaces, they are both in stable employment, and they have a cooperative and settled relationship with one another.

Studies have found that without these factors, equal time in shared care arrangements can be extremely stressful for everyone, but most detrimentally, is stressful for children.[51] If equal parenting time is important to you or to your children, developing a good, cooperative working relationship with your ex is the best place to start. You have to get the trust back into your interactions and it may take a great deal of concerted effort to get to a place of mutual respect and understanding. If that means turning the other cheek and laying down your weapons, then do it. This is not about you winning, this is about your child growing up without conflict and constant anxiety about how Mum and Dad will behave at the next soccer game or school event.

Rebekah reminds new clients that where there are no real protective concerns, the aim of the game is to be that family where the kids ultimately don't need to stress about inviting both parents to their wedding.

51 Bruce Smyth, Catherine Caruana and Anna Ferro, 'Fifty/fifty care: Parent-child contact and post-separation parenting arrangements', The Australian Institute of Family Studies, Research Report No. 9, July 2004.

Judges often express their frustration with parents who are too busy engaging in warfare to actually co-parent. Judge Coker of the Federal Circuit Court once wrote in a judgment:

> I have rarely been as disturbed by the comments that I have seen within family reports as I was by these comments. In a period of 18 months, the actions of these two apparently caring, loving and nurturing parents has torn the very fabric of their son's emotional wellbeing to shreds. Without a shadow of a doubt, they should both hang their heads in shame. They have both taken every possible step they could to score points against each other, and the absolute tragedy is that their son, to whom they profess the profoundest and deepest affection and love, has been the collateral damage.[52]

If your goal is to raise successful, healthy, loving children with the ability to maintain adult relationships, then both parties need to sometimes bite their tongue and turn the other cheek. The irony of highly conflictual parenting matters is that both parents are usually absolutely convinced that they are being the better parent and are 'fighting' for their children, when usually all they are doing is causing their children damage and spending money on legal fees that could be better spent on their children.

Sometimes, though, there are litigants who we family lawyers call 'the bad, the mad and the sad'. This is where one or both parties cannot be the Sane Parent. In these cases, no amount of cheek-turning and tongue-biting will help if the other parent, for whatever reason, cannot co-parent. Drug abuse, mental illness or just being a terrible person means that co-parenting is impossible. Co-parenting should not put your child or you at risk and prevention of that risk overrides the benefit of having a meaningful relationship in these cases.

What are the best plans for changeovers?

If you just can't get along, changeovers (where the child is 'handed over' from the care of one parent to the care of another) can be

52 Barnes & Abbey [2010] FamCA 1365 (3 December 2010) (paragraph 19).

an enormous source of stress and anxiety for both parents and the children. In some cases, where the parents have an angry divorce, it can be better to minimise all contact between the parents as much as possible. It is enormously damaging (and refer back to Sexton's report for more information on this) for a child to witness conflict between parents, particularly at a time when the child may already be experiencing stress at the prospect of leaving one parent.

Some parents are in such a state of war with one another (or one party is so afraid of the other) that changeovers have to be done in the carpark of the local police station, or in a public place, such as a McDonald's. If this can be avoided, then obviously that's best for everyone, but most especially it's best for the children that their family's dysfunction is on limited display to the public. Some families also utilise the services of a Children's Contact Service for supervised changeovers, which we'll talk about more a little later on.

If you are doing in-person changeovers, it's really important to minimise conflict as much as you can. It's horribly upsetting for the children to witness conflict or even cold rudeness between their parents. Here's some things to avoid:

- Videotaping the changeover on your mobile phone (unless you are specifically advised by your lawyer to do this), no matter how crucial you think the 'evidence' is. (This is much more common than you might think.)
- Taking the opportunity of being in the presence of your ex to make personal comments on their appearance, the state of the house or the garden, their new car, or their animals. Saying, 'Ew, your dog stinks' is rude and also, that's your kid's dog too.
- Ignoring your ex completely. Say hello and goodbye to your ex pleasantly. There's really no need for much more than that.
- Taking the opportunity to discuss difficult issues on the doorstep, or to dump unpleasant news on your ex (such as 'I've filed for full custody' or 'I'm engaged to my affair

partner'). Save that for later, preferably in writing, and possibly from your lawyer.

Basically, the only important thing to concentrate on during changeovers is your child or children. It's not a social call, unless you and your ex are actually friends. The kids are the focus—either say hello or goodbye to them at the door and then leave.

One way to limit interactions without the need for supervision is to design a parenting plan or consent orders whereby changeovers occur at school or daycare. This can be challenging, especially if the children are quite young, but there are ways around it.

Case study—John and Peta

John and Peta were married for eight years and now hated each other. Their divorce was absolutely toxic. They could not speak to one another without it degenerating into a vicious slanging match, and there were incidents of shoving between them. One time John shut the door on Peta's arm at a changeover, and another time Peta ran over John's foot. They had two children, Grace and Petra, aged five and seven.

Grace and Petra were in kindergarten and grade 1 at school. Every second weekend, they spent time with John. Because of the inability of John and Peta to communicate, they devised a schedule that limited their interactions. John picked the girls up from after-school care at 5 p.m. every second Friday, and dropped them back to before-school care by 8 a.m. the following Monday.

John and Peta used an app, called 2Houses, to communicate because they could not directly contact one another due to the animosity between them. The app ensured that communications were respectful and limited to matters relating to the children. Peta had a home phone that John could call the girls on between 6.30 and 7 each night, and Peta would not answer the phone during that time—Petra, the seven-year-old, would.

Other options can evolve over time, especially as the children grow older.

Case study—Sergio and Maria

Sergio and Maria could not get along. Maria absolutely despised Sergio. They had three children together, Marco, Michael and Bella, who were all in their early teens.

Each Wednesday night, the three children travelled to Sergio's house after school, and they had dinner with their father. After dinner, Sergio dropped the children back to Maria's house by 8.30 p.m. He would not go in the front gate.

Every second weekend, the children spent Friday and Saturday nights with Sergio, travelling to his house after school, and on Sunday at 5 p.m., Maria would pick the children up from Sergio's house. She would beep the horn to let the children know she had arrived, and would not go in the front gate.

Sergio and Maria communicated via email regarding the children, and Sergio could not contact Maria at all via iMessage or her phone (she blocked him). He communicated with the children directly, as they all had mobile phones.

Parallel parenting

This is a good option for very high-conflict divorces. Parallel parenting is the opposite of co-parenting, and is worth trying if you and your ex are constantly in a state of conflict, whether the conflict is over child-related matters or not, and you are both otherwise functional people.

Equal, shared parental responsibility is limited to 'major long-term issues' such as those relating to the child's education, name, religion, health matters or, for example, moving away so that the child's ability to see the other parent is impacted. Equal, shared parental responsibility does not mean that your child's other parent gets a say on how you run your home, or how you parent on a day-to-day basis. We know of one man who emailed his ex a twelve-page diatribe because she changed the brand of nappy she was using. This is not co-parenting, this is controlling your ex through your child.

In cases where you cannot co-parent, and where your ex is so angry and unreasonable (or you are) that your child is being exposed to conflict between parents, disengaging for a time (or forever) can be really helpful in terms of pressing the reset button, and giving you both some distance. As we know, the most damaging thing for a child to face after divorce is conflict between their parents.

Either parent can impose parallel parenting, and you do not need permission from your ex to do so; nor do you need to send inflammatory and dramatic emails advising the other parent that you are now parallel parenting and then going into a long diatribe detailing all of the other parent's many and various faults. (Don't forget this email will probably go into an affidavit and you will look crazy.)

There's no legal impediment to parallel parenting, as long as you consult with the other parent (even indirectly) on matters of 'shared parental responsibility' and follow the parenting plan or consent orders.

The key features of this approach are:

- The parenting plan or consent orders must be highly specific and must be stuck to rigorously. In parallel parenting, there's no room to ask one another for favours such as swapping days. All communication is indirect, and kept at a bare minimum, and verbal communication is not used at all—no talking on the phone, which can lead to shouting matches.
- No direct contact of any kind with one another. Many parents opt to use a parenting app, such as 2Houses, or Our Family Wizard. These apps (and there are several others) mean that you don't have to communicate via a phone-based messaging app (such as iMessage) or by email, which can greatly reduce conflict while still giving you a record of your discussions. These apps have, by and large, replaced the old-fashioned 'parenting notebooks', and can't get lost!

- In many cases, one parent may block the other parent from being able to contact them on their phones (most smartphones have this feature) and instead provide a third-party number for emergencies (such as the child's grandparent) who can then contact the other parent.
- If old enough, the children are given a phone that each parent can contact them on. Otherwise, each parent can contact the children on a designated number at a designated time and the children, not the parents, answer.
- In the most extreme cases, all communication is done between lawyers. A still extreme but less expensive option is to have all communications go through a third party, such as a grandparent or a close and trusted friend.
- Changeovers are done in a way whereby direct contact between parents is non-existent. The best way to do this is to make school, daycare or preschool the changeover point, so that one parent drops the child off in the morning after a contact period, and the other parent picks the child up in the afternoon (see also the section above on managing changeovers).
- Difficult, unavoidable discussions, such as about schooling choices, are had only with a third-party mediator present.

It's certainly possible for high-conflict divorces to gradually settle down as everyone moves on with their lives, so parallel parenting may not be needed forever. In the meantime, it can absolutely help in establishing appropriate boundaries and can definitely reduce conflict.

My child is refusing to go to their other parent's house—what are my options?

If you have consent orders or a court order, you must comply with the orders unless you have a reasonable belief that to do so will endanger you, or your child, or you have some other reasonable excuse, which we'll explain more later on. The court can make orders for children up until the child is aged eighteen, but in practice it's a bit of a different story, as we discussed earlier.

Sometimes, a young child will say that they don't want to go to Daddy's house, or they don't want to go to Mummy's house. This can be very upsetting for the 'rejected' parent, but as always, communication is key. As gratifying as it may be for the 'chosen' parent, it's usually not in the child's best interests to refuse to spend time with both of their parents and it's your job as the parent to get to the bottom of why your kid doesn't want to spend time with your ex.

You wouldn't let your child choose not to go to school, and going to their other parent's house is similarly not generally optional. If there are consent or court orders in place, there can be serious consequences if your child doesn't go to their other parent's house as set out in the orders, unless there is a reasonable excuse. A reasonable excuse may be that your child was at school camp, or was hospitalised, or was bedridden with the flu and you've got the doctor's certificate to prove it, and you notified your ex of this in writing.

In cases of refusal, you can ask non-leading questions to find out your child's reasons (such as 'Can you tell me why you don't want to go, so we can figure it out together?' rather than 'It's because he never spends any time with you without that skanky ho[53] following him everywhere, isn't it?').

It's important, obviously, to get to the bottom of refusals, because sometimes it can be for not-very-nice factors, which we'll discuss at the end of the following list.

Refusal can be for a range of reasons:

- A mismatch in parenting styles, where one parent is very lax and the other is very authoritarian, so the child is confused about acceptable behaviour in either house, or just frankly prefers the house where they are allowed to stay up late gaming, eat junk food, and not have to go to school if they don't want to.

53 Calling your ex's new partner names is not exactly being the Sane Parent, as tempting as it may undoubtedly be.

- An attachment issue, where a child is very anxious and fearful away from their primary attachment figure (generally the mother, although not always).
- A lack of quality time together, especially where households are busy with step-parents and step-siblings and other siblings, chores and weekend sport—it's easy for one kid to slip beneath the radar and feel left out and alone.
- The child may sleep with Mummy in her bed but isn't allowed to share a bed at Daddy's, or the child may share a bedroom with a sibling in one house and love it/or hate it, and may want/not want that same situation at their other house.
- A great deal of animosity between parents, so that the child feels guilty for leaving Mummy or Daddy.
- The child misses their other parent unbearably when they are away, and the period away is too long. In these cases, by being a bit more flexible and a bit more sensitive to what your child is trying to tell you, you'll actually improve your relationship with your child far more than an extra night a fortnight ever would.
- Their needs aren't being met by the parent when the child is with them (such as Daddy spending all day in bed or Mummy talking on the phone too much).
- Little things, like the other parent having a scary cat or a mean neighbour, or hurting the child while brushing their hair, can build up into huge and valid things in the child's mind.
- A child feels like they need to tell both parents that they don't want to go to the other parent at the end of each changeover—especially in highly conflictual separations, the child is telling both parents what the child thinks that parent wants to hear. This means the child is pretty much always anxious about leaving either parent and loves both parents.

- Or, sometimes, it can be for big things—neglect, abuse, bullying, violence—all the horrible things we don't want to think about, and are not necessarily perpetrated by the other parent, but by other people your child comes into contact with in their home.

Once you've gotten to the bottom of the issues driving the refusal, you can attempt to work with your ex on what the problem is. (Isn't that going to be a fun conversation?!) For example, your child might simply want to spend more one-on-one time with their other parent, and might need to be made to feel a bit more special. Or, they might need to have access to snacks between meals. They might need to break up the visit a bit by seeing Mummy after school one day, or for a milkshake on Saturday morning. Or both parents may need to let the child know it is okay to go to the other parent, that Mummy or Daddy won't be sitting around pining for them and crying.

By acting in the child's best interests, not according to what the parent wants, refusals can often be addressed so that the child chooses to go. Making a small child go kicking and screaming to their other parent isn't good for anyone, let alone the poor kid, and isn't going to do much for parent and child bonding. However, sometimes the issue is not spending time with the other parent but the actual changeover itself. Usually your child will be absolutely fine within ten minutes. You may remember your child's first few weeks at daycare or school—when they were sobbing uncontrollably as you left but were fine pretty much as soon as you had gone. Rebekah remembers sitting in the carpark at daycare trying to compose herself after her eldest was hanging onto the gate sobbing, 'Mummy, Mummy please don't go', then ringing the centre, to be told, 'Oh, she's fine; in fact, she was fine as soon as you left, she's happily playing with her friends now'. Changeovers can be the same and it is the job of both parents to work through this with the child.

Rather than clinging to your child for last kisses, more last kisses, one last kiss because 'Mummy/Daddy will miss you soooo much' or showing your child that you are crying or about to cry, say goodbye cheerfully and let your child know it is okay for them to love and spend time with their other parent. Do this in both words and actions.

This is one of those times where you both need to be the adults and reassure your child. Rebekah dealt with her clingy and anxious child by cheerily saying at changeover, 'Okay, bye-bye, Mummy is off now, have fun with Daddy'.

If, however, the reason for refusal is a big, horrible thing, then your first port of call should be your lawyer. You don't have to send your child anywhere if there is a reasonable belief that they will be unsafe—in fact, you shouldn't. But in this situation the key word is 'reasonable', and what feels reasonable to you may not stack up in court. You must consult with your lawyer urgently, especially if you have court orders, because otherwise you could be in breach of them and there can be some very serious consequences to breaching orders, as we've discussed earlier.

If you do have court orders that provide for the children to live with or spend time with their other parent, then you have to be proactive in making that happen. The family law courts have put out a helpful (no, really) brochure called 'Parenting Orders: Obligations, Consequences and Who Can Help' and it says:

> You cannot be merely passive but must take positive action and this positive obligation includes taking all reasonable steps to ensure that the order is put into effect. You must also positively encourage your children to comply with the orders. For example where the order states your children are to spend time with another party, you must not only ensure that the children are available but must also positively encourage them to go and do so.

The brochure (which you can also find online[54]) details places where you can get help if there are difficulties in getting the kids to go to see their other parent, such as Family Relationships Online (www.familyrelationships.gov.au) or a Family Relationship Centre. Other help is available, such as from a child psychologist or a

54 www.familycourt.gov.au/wps/wcm/connect/fcoaweb/reports-and-publications/publications/court-orders/parenting-orders-obligations-consequences-and-who-can-help.

school counsellor, who can help parents get to the bottom of the problem together.

You must also be aware that if you do not actively support your children's right to know and be cared for by their other parent, then the courts can and do make orders that the children live with their other parent.

Case study—Martina and Jonah

Martina and Jonah separated after a brief, three-year marriage. They had two children, James and Lily, who were aged two and four at the time of the separation and were now aged eight and ten. Martina was not a fan of Jonah, who had remarried and had two more children.

Since the separation, James and Lily had lived with Martina, who was an attentive and involved mother. She organised many after-school activities for the children, who went to excellent schools, were always on time to class, and had close, attached relationships with their mother.

The children were supposed to spend time with their father every second weekend and for half of the school holidays. He was considered by the court to be a 'good enough parent' who didn't particularly want the children to live with him, but did want to spend time with them.

However, Martina did not take active steps to foster a positive relationship between the children and their father. In fact, Martina made it clear that she would prefer the children did not have a relationship with Jonah at all. She often organised activities, such as family camping trips, on the weekends the children were supposed to be with their father, and put the children in the position where they had to choose where they would go for the weekend. She also made it clear to the children that she did not like their father ringing the house to talk to them. James, in particular, had a very difficult relationship with his father and had made allegations of abuse against him, which were not substantiated.

The matter went to a full hearing of the Family Court. After a five-day hearing, the court ordered that James and Lily live with their father full time, and further ordered that the children only have supervised contact with their mother for two hours a fortnight for a period of no less than six months.

The court found that even though the separation of the children from their mother would be extremely difficult for the children, it considered that the risk of a total breakdown of a relationship with their father was more damaging in the long term.

Supervised time and changeovers

As we've discussed throughout this book, the court almost always takes the view that a child knowing both of their parents is really important. The major factors that the court must consider are the benefit to the child of having a meaningful relationship with both parents; and any need to protect the child from abuse, neglect or family violence, or being exposed to abuse, neglect or family violence. If there is a need to protect a child, then this has to be given more weight.

Sometimes, issues can get in the way of a parent being able to care for their child unsupervised, even for short periods of time. This might include allegations or findings of violent behaviour by a parent towards a child or another person, allegations or findings of serious drug or alcohol abuse, or long periods of absence by a parent from a child's life.

The court can order that a child spend supervised time with a parent at a contact centre. The court can also order that changeovers be supervised. Parents can agree to use a contact centre and this is not uncommon when a parent wants to re-establish a relationship with a child, especially if that relationship was interrupted because the parent was in jail or rehabilitation.

The federal government funds Children's Contact Service providers across Australia. They are designed to be safe, fun places for children, and the people supervising the contact between the child and the parent are trained in helping ensure that the time is spent in a happy, child-focused way. The details and locations of contact centres can be found at the Australian Children's Contact Services Association website at www.accsa.org.au. There can be very long waiting lists at the contact centres.

There are also private organisations, such as Dial-An-Angel, LifeCare and Kindred Connect, who provide contact centre services. These organisations can be expensive but usually do not have the lengthy waiting lists that the publicly funded contact centres have. This can be a good option for short-term supervised contact, such as when a brief period of reconnection is needed.

While the Children's Contact Service is funded by the government, fees will often still apply. Parents on low incomes can seek assistance to access the service by applying to the service provider. More information can be found at www.familyrelationships.gov.au/BrochuresandPublications/Pages/supervised-visits-and-changeovers.aspx.

Generally the idea of supervised time is to reduce and eventually eliminate the need for supervision, but quite often parents agree to other forms of informal supervision, such as the parent staying with a grandparent during contact times if there are any residual or ongoing concerns (such as mental health or drug problems that might impact on the capacity of a parent to fully care for their child). The aim should usually be to get to the point where the parent and child can safely spend time together unsupervised. For some families, that point may never arrive, and supervised time can be a great way to ensure that the child doesn't completely miss out on the opportunity to know their parent.

It can be confronting to hear a court ordering that your child spend time with you at a contact centre. The court generally makes supervision orders on a temporary basis, whether until a child becomes more comfortable with their parent, until a parent is able to provide clean drug screen results, or until a family report is available. The court has to be cautious and may make an order that you think is really unfair—and it may be really unfair. Sometimes when in this position, a parent will decide to stop participating in the court process, or even worse, in their child's life.

If you are faced with this situation, it is important to hang in there. Simply withdrawing will just make things worse and will deprive your child of their right to have a meaningful relationship with both parents, and can lead to a devastating rupture in your relationship with your child that may never be repaired. As difficult as it is, as our teenagers would say, sometimes you just have to cop it for your kid.

No time orders

In very unusual cases, an order will be made that a child spend no time with a parent. This sort of order is made when the risk to a child is greater than the benefit to the child of a meaningful relationship and there is no way to reduce the risk (such as supervision or period of being subject to ongoing drug testing—and returning clean results).

Nobody wins in these cases, and they are often the most devastating ones to work on as a family lawyer (not that it's all about us). However, sometimes there's no other possible outcome, and the safety of the children must come first.

Parental abandonment

Sometimes, after separation, a parent turns out to be even more selfish than you'd ever thought possible, and abandons their children. This can be total abandonment (such that the parent just never sees the child again) or sporadic abandonment, where the parent sees the child when it suits them.

As we've discussed before, the courts can order a child to spend time with a parent but can't (and won't) make a parent spend time with the child. While child support and spending time together are totally separate things at law (which means you can't deny contact because your ex hasn't paid their child support), it's quite common for a parent to skip out on the child and show enormous reluctance to pony up the cash as well (by doing cash jobs, or being underemployed, for example).

Parental abandonment is absolutely horrible, for both the child and the parent left holding the baby. There's never a good reason to abandon your child, and no, the difficulties and challenges of the family law system don't excuse it. We're so sorry if you're experiencing this. It's awful to not be able to talk to your child's other parent, the only person on earth who should love them as much as you do, about your kid.

It's very difficult for the child and they will need a great deal of support to help them deal with it. Counselling is crucial in these cases. If money is short (not least because of the deadbeat other parent), then school counsellors are a great place to start, as is a mental health plan from your GP.

Disputes over international travel and passports

This is a very common area of conflict between separated parents. And boy, is it a tough one.

In Chapter 1, we discussed international parental abduction. It's such an important issue we put it right at the front of the book. In this section, we're going to talk about international travel with children in a bit more detail, and what your options are.

As you probably know, without a court order it is difficult to get a passport issued for a child if the other parent won't consent to it. It's also common for one parent to put the children on an airport 'watch list' so that the other parent can't leave the country with the children even if they do have passports.

There are generally two issues at play here. The first issue is your garden-variety attempt at control. By refusing to let you take the kids to Bali for a week,[55] your ex is still having a very big say in your life and they're basically trapping you in Australia, possibly for the next eighteen years. While not being able to go on overseas holidays is by definition a First World problem, it's still upsetting and annoying.

The second issue is more serious. One parent may have real and warranted concerns about the possibility that the other parent will leave the country with the children and not return. As we discussed

55 Which is not in a Hague Convention country, just FYI.

earlier, getting your children back in this situation is expensive at best and utterly impossible at worst, depending on the country. The publicity regarding a failed attempt in 2016 to recover children from Lebanon was heartbreaking and scary.

In matters such as these, parents often self-represent. It's not that hard to self-represent, and there are many online resources that can help guide you through step by step (in addition to this one, of course!)

In the first instance, you can make a special circumstances application to the Passport Office for a passport to be issued to your child without the other parent's agreement. This is usually only granted in cases where there are orders allowing international travel or the other parent has disappeared off the face of the earth, and you've made substantial efforts to locate them.

Otherwise, if your ex simply won't agree to your children being issued a passport, or being allowed to travel internationally, you will have to apply to the court for an order. This is actually quite a common application but it can take a very long time to progress through the system. The court will consider the case on its merits and make an order one way or the other. This involves assessing the risk of failing to return the child to Australia and the benefits of visiting the other country.

In one case we know of, the mother had not told the court about any particular benefits of the child visiting her home country and had, at separation, apparently offered the father money if he agreed to allow her to take the child to live in that country. The mother did not address this allegation in her affidavit, and so was taken to have not denied the allegation. The mother did offer security in the form of funds of $200 000 against her not returning, but had not set out whether this was enough to allow the father to pursue recovery through the courts in the other country, or sufficient motivation for her to return. The assessment of the court was that:

> In assessing the risk of detriment ... the potential loss of meaningful relationship with the father and the benefits that may flow from that against the potential benefits to the child in allowing the

> travel ... at this stage the child's interests are not supported by allowing the mother to travel with her to Country D.[56]

If you are from a non–Hague Convention country (and see Chapter 1 for more information about what the Hague Convention is), have had an incredibly nasty divorce, have extensive family in your home country, and have lined up a job there, the answer from the court as to whether you can take the kids on a holiday back home will probably be no.

If, however, you are from a non–Hague Convention country and have substantial ties to Australia, such as a home, job and superannuation, and have actively supported a relationship between the child and their other parent, then the answer may be yes but you may be required to provide security in the form of cash.

The risk assessment may change over time. In one matter Rebekah was involved in, the judge at first did not allow the mother to travel to her home country with the child. The country was not a signatory to the Hague Convention. By the final hearing, the judge found that the mother had significant ties to Australia, including money in the bank, superannuation, a good job that she liked and a partner who also had a good job. The child had been talking to her grandparents in the other country by Skype and there was medical evidence before the court showing that the elderly grandparents were not able to travel to Australia. Despite quite a lot of nastiness from the father, the mother had continued to support the child's relationship with him. The judge found that given all of these circumstances it was more likely than not that the mother would return to Australia with the child, and the mother did just that after a lovely visit to her family.

Sometimes a teenager wants to go overseas without their parents. If your child has been chosen to go for a school excursion overseas (and done the fundraising) or to Paris with their much-loved grandmother, and you say no without a good reason, expect both the judge and your teenager to be deeply unhappy. While really all the judge can do is make orders (possibly including that you

56 Koyroyshs & Koyroyshs [2016] FamCA 1046 (7 December 2016) (paragraph 20).

pay the costs of the other party) against you, it is likely that the damage done to the relationship with your child will be immense and unnecessary.

As with all disputes over parenting choices, mediation is often a great way to resolve these issues, which are one of the most common reasons parents return to mediation after their matter has been finalised.

Sole parental responsibility

As we know, the Family Law Act presumes that it is in the child's best interests for parents to have 'equal shared parental responsibility' for their child or children. However, in some cases this presumption does not apply, such as when there is proven family violence, and when the child has been subjected to abuse by the other parent.

In other cases, shared parental responsibility is a 'rebuttable presumption'—that is, either parent (or sometimes both) can put forward their arguments as to why the other parent should not have shared parental responsibility. You have to do this by applying for an order of the court. The assumption of shared responsibility can only be rebutted in a limited number of circumstances. It's not something that the courts will agree to lightly.

Sole parental responsibility is usually granted to a parent in circumstances where the other parent is unable to easily communicate with the parent (for example, the other parent is in jail for a lengthy period of time). Or where it would not be in the best interests of the child for the parents to share parental responsibility, whether because one parent does not have the capacity to make decisions (this could be due to a brain injury, or drug use or a mental illness) or due to intractable conflict (when parents cannot agree on anything at all and the chances of them ever agreeing in the future are vanishingly small).

The last point is generally the most difficult application to make to the court. The court expects parents to behave like adults, but sometimes, for whatever reason, the relationship between the parents has completely broken down to the point that the court judges it to be unsalvageable.

Or it may be that the parents have such contrary and strongly held views, over very important matters such as the child's religion or a decision to medicate or vaccinate the child, that it is not in the child's best interests for the parents to continue to try to resolve their differences, because it becomes clear that this will not be possible.

Case study—Amit and Raia

Amit and Raia had been married for fifteen years. They had two children, Anja, who was twelve and Muhammad, who was ten.

A significant dispute between the parents arose over Amit's desire that Anja wear a hijab as she approached puberty, and that she only associate with other children of her religion, by going to a particular school. Raia, who did wear a hijab, wanted the decision to be Anja's alone, and did not want her children to only associate with other children of the same religion. She wanted the children to remain at the same secular school.

These and other issues lead to Amit and Raia separating. Raia applied to the court to have sole parental responsibility of Anja and Muhammad because of Amit's very strongly held views, which were so contrary to hers that she felt agreement could not be reached.

The court ruled in Raia's favour and granted her sole parental responsibility for the children.

Sole parental responsibility doesn't necessarily mean that the parent without responsibility will also be denied the opportunity to spend time with the child. It doesn't mean sole parenting—it just means that it's in the best interests of the child that only one parent make the decisions in relation to major issues. Often, even if a parent has sole parental responsibility, that parent must first ask the other parent for input into the decision to be made, and must take that input into account when making the decision.

Sole parental responsibility can also be granted over certain issues. This means, for example, that a parent may be granted the sole responsibility to make decisions relating to the health of a child.

Disputes over medical treatment

Another hotbed of acrimony between separated parents is the reality of having to make medical decisions together.

Deciding on surgery or a course of treatment, or, even more heartbreakingly, making the decision to cease treatment for your child, when there are conflicting opinions between doctors and between parents is incredibly difficult. So difficult, in fact, that sometimes the court has to decide. Mediation, of course, can help. Common disputes are over:

- medical issues that are largely cosmetic but are upsetting for the child (such as sticky-out ears or a prominent nose)
- experimental procedures that may not have a tangible, proven benefit to the child
- continuing cancer treatment or ceasing cancer treatment and moving on to hospice care
- removing teeth for orthodontic procedures
- other non-emergency procedures.

If your child is faced with an operation or procedure, consent is a slightly or possibly hugely tricky issue if you're separated. Older children may be able to consent to medical treatment (including birth control) themselves. The term is often called 'Gillick' competency, after a case in England where Mrs Gillick wanted an assurance from her area health service that no doctor would prescribe contraception to any of her daughters without her consent until they were eighteen. The area health service had put out a circular stating that doctors could prescribe contraception to a child under sixteen without parental consent and that it was a matter of the doctor's discretion. The English House of Lords found that: 'As a matter of Law the parental right to determine whether or not their minor child below the age of sixteen will have medical treatment terminates if and when the child achieves sufficient understanding and intelligence to understand fully what is proposed.[57]

57 Gillick v. West Norfolk and Wisbech AHA [1985] UKHL 7.

The High Court in Marion's case[58] held that Gillick is law in Australia as well, stating that: 'A minor is ... capable of giving informed consent when he or she achieves a sufficient understanding and intelligence to enable him or her to understand fully what is proposed.' New South Wales and South Australia have legislation covering the age that a child can give consent (fourteen and sixteen respectively).[59]

As we've discussed, the family law courts can give both parents shared parental responsibility over medical decisions, or can decide that one parent only can make decisions relating to the child's medical needs. There have to be pretty good reasons for the family law courts to take this responsibility away from one parent and give it solely to the other, and it's generally for reasons such as one parent holding such extreme views that the court decides they are incapable of making reasonable decisions with the other parent.

It's also common for one parent to try to exert control over the other parent by obsessing over the health of the child, or by being overly critical of the pretty reasonable choices being made by the other parent when they are caring for the child, such as giving vitamins or cough medicine, or using a certain brand of lotion instead of some other brand. We know of one case where one parent actually wanted an itemised list of all the pharmaceutical products the child (who was twelve) had ingested over five days when the child had a cold. The list, when supplied, comprised children's Panadol and over-the-counter eucalyptus cough drops. To be clear, these are not major long-term 'medical' decisions, they are day-to-day 'parenting' decisions. It's a form of very nasty bullying when one parent tries to control the other parent like this.

Another really difficult topic is vaccinations, when one parent wants to vaccinate and the other is vehemently opposed. Regardless of how we as lawyers feel about these beliefs, there can be little doubt that among some parents they are very strongly and genuinely

58 Secretary, Department of Health and Community Services v. J.W.B. AND S.M.B. (Marion's case) [1992] HCA 15; (1992) 175 CLR 218.

59 Section 49 (2) *Minors (Property and Contracts) Act 1970* (NSW); Section 6(1) *Consent to Medical and Dental Procedures Act* 1985 (SA).

held, and it's not unknown for one parent to disappear with a child in order to prevent vaccinations. (Rebekah used to practise family law near Byron Bay, where this occurred.)

Again, if mediation fails, a parent can apply to the court to order that the child be vaccinated, but the court won't order that a child not be vaccinated unless there is a very compelling medical reason why not, such as the child has a greatly weakened immune system. This requires medical evidence from someone properly qualified to give it. Only experts can give evidence of opinion and the opinion must be based on their particular expertise using the methodology that is appropriate to the question at hand.[60]

Special medical procedures

The Family Court has a special jurisdiction in matters involving medical procedures such as gender reassignment for minors, sterilisation of minors, and matters where there is no parental consent given for lifesaving treatment. There are also state laws that cover sterilisation of minors and lifesaving treatment. This is a fascinating area of law and ethics but not something that we can cover in any detail here.

There is some controversy regarding whether gender reassignment should have to be the subject of an application to the court, as the vast majority, if not all, medical professionals working in this field are not only experts, but are ethical and sensible as well.

Sterilisation of minors with a disability is a complex matter and has to be decided upon on a case-by-case basis. Ethical issues regarding the right of a person to have control over their own reproductive decisions have to be balanced with the capacity of the child to make the decision and deal with the consequences of the decision—whether now or in the future. To make a decision that a child undergo invasive surgery to deprive them of the ability to have a baby is not a decision that could ever be made lightly.

The family law courts can be asked to make an order that a child have lifesaving treatment in cases where one or both parents are refusing to give consent. The hospital or a parent can bring the

60 Makita (Australia) Pty Ltd v. Sprowles [2001] NSWCA 305 (14 September 2001).

application. If there are court orders providing for shared parental responsibility for medical issues, and a parent does not consent, then an application to the court can be made in circumstances of urgency, and generally this will be heard immediately (and usually your lawyer will have chosen that day of all days to wear jeans to the office).

The court is most likely to act with caution and to order that the parent consenting to medical treatment has sole parental responsibility for that issue, unless some very compelling medical evidence from an appropriately qualified medical practitioner backing up the non-consenting parent is available. As we mentioned previously when talking about vaccinations, only experts can give evidence of opinion and the opinion must be based on their particular expertise using the methodology appropriate to the question at hand.[61]

The court will overrule religious concerns (such as those held by Jehovah's Witnesses regarding blood products) if a child needs urgent medical treatment, even if the child also withholds their consent.

Choosing your child's name

Choosing your child's name (including the first name and the last name) can be hard for couples who are still together, and for couples who have split up before or shortly after a baby is born, it can be a minefield. If parents cannot choose a name, then an application can be made to the family law courts or to the registrar of Births Deaths and Marriages, who can assign the child a name.

In one case, the judge said that her approach was to let the parents know that if they could not agree, she would call the child Susan if a girl or Peter if a boy. She would then send them outside for one last chance to agree. Apparently there are quite a few Susans and Peters around as a result.

There are limitations on registering names and in most states these include:

- names that are obscene or offensive
- names that are too long

61 Makita's case.

- names that include symbols without phonetic significance
- names that are ranks or titles, such as Princess or General (so no Major Major Major Major)
- a name being, for example, contrary to the public interest, such as 'Hitler' or 'Bonghead' (no, seriously).

A child lumped with a problematic name can always ask the court to change it. In New Zealand, a judge who was asked by a child to change her name from Talulah Does the Hula From Hawaii said: 'The court is profoundly concerned about the very poor judgment that this child's parents have shown in choosing this name. It makes a fool of the child and sets her up with a social disability and handicap, unnecessarily.'[62]

The New Zealand judge further said that names like Stallion, Yeah Detroit, Fish and Chips, Twisty Poi, Keenan Got Lucy and Sex Fruit had been prohibited by New Zealand registry officials,[63] meaning that these were names that people had *tried* to register for their children. The Swedish Government said no to @ Brfxxccxxmnpcccclllmmnprxvclmnckssqlbb11116, the Danes were not having Anus, and the registrar in the state of Victoria decided Satan was not on, but apparently New South Wales did allow Fully Hektik Sik.[64]

Changing your child's name

Applying for a change of a child's name (either first name, last name, or both—or even middle names, we suppose) is done through Births Deaths and Marriages in the state in which the child was born. Changing a child's name is not an exercise to be embarked upon lightly. In most states, *usually* if both parents are named on the birth certificate, then the registrar of Births Deaths and Marriages will require that both parents sign the application before a qualified witness. In Western Australia, if both parents have signed the

62 www.theguardian.com/lifeandstyle/2008/jul/24/familyandrelationships.newzealand.

63 ibid.

64 www.news.com.au/lifestyle/parenting/babies/victorian-government-releases-list-of-banned-baby-names/news-story/8a2f110daf7de8800ca555dbc48e47cc.

application for a birth certificate, then both will need to sign the application for a change of name.

If a parent who is named on the birth certificate does not consent to a change of name, then a court order will be necessary. Your child's name is defined in the Family Law Act as a 'major long-term issue' and if there are court orders saying that you and your ex have shared parental responsibility for the children, then you must consult with your ex before changing your child's name. If you and your ex cannot agree, you will need to make an application to the court.

If the child is over twelve, then they will need to consent to the change in name and sign the form in front of a witness.

If both parents are not named on the birth certificate, the parent not named on the birth certificate can still apply to the family law courts (usually the Federal Circuit Court) to stop the other parent from changing the child's name.

An application can also be made to the family law courts to stop a parent from informally using another name for a child—just adopting another name despite what the birth certificate says. This includes filling out forms (enrolling the child in, say, dance classes) with a different name from the name on the child's birth certificate.

There are some limitations on how many times a child's name can be changed (you can't change it three times in two years, for example), and in some states there are also limitations on changing the name of a child if an order has provided that the director-general of a state child protection agency has parental responsibility, or if the child is under the supervision of correctional services, a mental health review tribunal, or is a registered sex offender.

When considering an application to change a child's name, the court will generally consider:

- the welfare of the child, which is the paramount consideration
- the short- and long-term effects of any change in the child's surname

- any embarrassment likely to be experienced by the child if the child's name is different from that of the parent with whom the child lives
- any confusion of identity that may arise for the child if their name is changed or is not changed
- the effect any change in surname may have on the relationship between the child and the parent whose name the child bore during the marriage
- the effect of frequent or random changes of name.[65]

As we have discussed, even if you and the other parent agree to a change of name, the registrar of Births Deaths and Marriages in your state will not allow a child's name to be changed to a prohibited name (so Princess Consuela Banana Hammock is probably out, and Crap Bag definitely is).

I want to move away so that I can afford to buy a new house but my ex says I can't

Relocation cases (that is, where one parent wants to move away from the other parent) are notoriously difficult to predict in terms of outcomes. When lawyers talk about 'bad, mad or sad' cases, relocation cases are often the 'sad' cases. Often, two parents are perfectly good parents, the children love both parents and the parents have very good reasons for wanting to live thousands of kilometres apart.

When deciding on relocation cases the court's paramount consideration is still the best interests of the child. Each case depends on the unique circumstances of the matter. Generally speaking, the court may find that moving a distance of an hour away is acceptable, but if it means changing schools or spending much less time with the other parent, it becomes a more difficult proposition.

This can be crazy-making for the parent who is trying to rehouse themselves. Feeling 'stuck' and having an ex controlling where you can live is the number one complaint of the vast majority of

65 In the marriage of Chapman, AL & Palmer, RJ [1978] FamCA 86.

separated women who find themselves priced out of the property market post-separation (and in these cases, it's usually the woman).

On the other hand, it can be very upsetting for a parent (often the father) to lose substantial day-to-day contact with his children if their mother moves away. These are very difficult cases. The court tries to determine them on a 'least worst' outcome basis, and the wishes of the child will be taken into account.

Case study—Rachel and Mark

Rachel and Mark had one child together, Emily, aged twelve. They had been separated for four years, and Mark cared for Emily every second weekend and for half of the school holidays. This arrangement was working well and Emily was happily settled and in her last year of primary school.

Rachel announced that she had purchased a new home for her and Emily, in a smaller town two hours drive away. She told Mark that she would still facilitate his time with Emily, by meeting him halfway every second Friday and Sunday, and the same again for his holiday contact periods.

Emily was greatly opposed to the move. She wished to go to the local high school with all her friends. Mark's preference was that Rachel remained living with Emily in their current town, but as an alternative, proposed that Emily live with him and spend time with Rachel.

The court found in the interim that Mark's work roster would not allow him to provide as much personal care of Emily as Rachel currently did, and would continue to do, in the new town.

It also found that the distance wasn't so great as to endanger the continued relationship between father and daughter (and indeed Mark did not seem greatly perturbed by the two-hour round trip). The decision said that while much weight could be given to Emily's wishes, her interests were best served by remaining with her mother.

So we can see that in this case, the court found that the benefits of Emily remaining in the predominant care of her mother, despite the move and despite Emily's opposition, outweighed the drawbacks, especially as Emily wasn't going to be losing time with her dad.

Generally speaking, the court will consider issues such as:

- the best interests of the child
- the benefit to the child of having a meaningful relationship with both of their parents
- the need to protect the child from physical or psychological harm from being subjected to, or exposed to, abuse, neglect or family violence
- the practical difficulty and expense of a child spending time with and communicating with a parent, and whether that difficulty or expense will substantially affect the child's right to maintain personal relations and direct contact with both parents on a regular basis
- the distance the parent wishes to move (and what impact that will have on the child's relationship with both of their parents)
- the capacity of both parents to properly care for the child
- the child's wishes.

Going to court on relocation matters is often very expensive—it can cost well over $40 000 per party, with no guarantees as to outcomes. As always, giving mediation the very best shot you can, and being open to compromise, can save you a lot of time and stress. Sometimes, however, no matter how willing to compromise you are, your ex just won't—and in these cases, going to court becomes inevitable.

Mediation

In family law matters in Australia, the word 'mediator' has been replaced with 'family dispute resolution provider'.

As lawyers, we like acronyms and can have lengthy conversations made up entirely of acronyms. However, our loved ones have pointed out that no one else can understand us and we sound like total idiots (although we think the technical word they used was 'tossers'). So in the interests of not using four words when one commonly understood word will do, or even worse, using an acronym—FDRP—we will just use the word 'mediator'.

Going to court for parenting matters generally only happens after you've been to mediation that either was not successful or only partially successful. This is because usually you need a mediation certificate (called a section 60I certificate) from the mediator to say that, in their opinion, you have tried but there's not much chance of the two of you reaching an agreement, or that the matter was not suitable, or one party refused to go.

A mediator has to be satisfied that a matter is suitable for mediation, and in parenting matters, they look at factors such as:

- a history of family violence, if any (and see the Glossary), among the parties
- the likely safety of the parties
- the equality of bargaining power among the parties
- the risk that a child may suffer abuse
- the emotional, psychological and physical health of the parties
- any other matter that the mediator (and see the Glossary) considers relevant to the proposed family dispute resolution.

Do not refuse to go to the intake (which is the legal term for the first appointment with the mediator or mediation service), as there could be serious consequences for you later if your ex asks for costs. This is where you are forced by law to pay the costs of your ex if you lose or vice versa. It can end up costing you a lot of money (that's why we call it costs, 'cause it's gonna cost ya).

An intake appointment is just you and someone from the mediation service, so your ex will not be there. This appointment is where you let the mediator know if there are any barriers to negotiating freely with your ex, so the mediator can assess whether the matter is suitable for mediation or not. The mediator may suggest that the matter is suitable for mediation only on the condition that it is telephone mediation, 'shuttle' mediation or if a support person is present.

It is actually quite amazing what a skilled mediator can achieve. Rebekah has gone into mediations where the parties are so far apart in what they saw as an acceptable outcome that she thought negotiating Middle Eastern peace would have been an easier way to spend the day. But an experienced and patient mediator can perform near miracles, and going into mediation with an open mind can be a helpful starting point. You never know, you and your ex may both have a sudden attack of the reasonables, and finalise all the major decisions then and there.

Private mediation can be expensive (although not as expensive as going to court—and see more on court fees in this chapter). Generally, you and your ex will be expected to split the costs, which can be up to $5500 a day (for a six-hour mediation) if you use a private mediator.

You can also use a publicly subsidised mediation service, through the federal government's Family Relationship Centres, which provides one hour of meditation free, and two hours after that for $30 an hour (some income tests apply). Family Relationship Centres can be found at www.familyrelationships.gov.au/Services.

Types of mediation

Face to face

If you and your ex get along fairly well and there has been no violence or abuse in the relationship, face-to-face mediation can be invaluable. Sitting down and working through issues with a trained mediator usually means that outcomes are not only suitable for both parties (or both parties can at least live with them) but the co-parenting relationship is at best strengthened and at worst not destroyed utterly. Parties can get stuff off their chests that bothers them, in a respectful environment, and this can include issues that will not be ventilated in court because they are not of any interest to anybody in a courtroom setting.

Usually face-to-face mediation will follow the National Mediator Accreditation System (NMAS) practice standards and include:

- intake (which is an introductory session where you get to cry and gnash your teeth and wail, and then pull yourself together as best you can)
- a joint session where the mediator lets you all know why you are there
- opening statements by the parties
- agenda-setting by the parties
- private sessions
- exploration of agenda
- generating solutions
- finalising the agreement.

Telephone mediation

This can work really well, as it lets both parties process information without the stress of the other party being physically present. It also lets parties who live far apart from each other mediate, and caters for parties who live in remote areas without other mediation services. The Family Relationship Advice Line can organise telephone mediation.[66] The telephone mediation process is much the same as the face-to-face process, just on the telephone. Some private mediators are offering Skype mediation as well.

Shuttle mediation

This is where the parties are in a separate room for all or for the majority of the mediation and the mediator goes between the rooms. It's a great option if you're really not comfortable being in the same room as your ex, especially if they have a tendency to try to bully

66 www.familyrelationships.gov.au/Services/FRAL/Pages/default.aspx.

you, or if you just don't particularly want to spend six hours sitting across the table from them. In some ways, shuttle mediation can be even more effective than face to face because the mediator, not you, is relaying your responses, which takes a lot of the emotion out of the whole thing.

Facilitative

This is a structured mediation style where the mediator acts as a kind of referee rather than providing options to the parties or giving an opinion on the options generated by the parties. The NMAS sets out a highly structured way of conducting mediations, which usually goes like this:

Mediator's opening statement

The mediator firstly talks about why you are here. The mediator sets out the rules (such as no talking over each other and no threatening each other, most of which are ignored in the first three minutes and then have to be restated again and again), the limited circumstances where information from a mediation may be used against you (such as if you disclose that you're divorcing your ex because they literally murdered someone), the confidentiality of the mediation, how to make a complaint about the mediator, how any agreements can be formalised and where the toilets are, and if you have to evacuate, whether it's on the whoop whoop or on the beep beep.

Parties' opening statement

This is where you get to tell the mediator and each other why you are here and what you actually want. It helps to have thought about that before you go to mediation. The mediator will adopt LARSQ, which is an awesome acronym (so exciting!) and means listening, acknowledging, reframing, summarising and questioning.[67] The mediator will listen to you, acknowledge the

67 In the marriage of Chapman, AL & Palmer, RJ [1978] FamCA 86.

issue you wish to discuss, 'reframe' your words, summarise the issue and check with you they have it right.

Reframing is a bit of an art and a good mediator will work out from your statement what the issue is that you want to resolve and then make it a neutral statement, so that it is capable of exploration and hopefully resolution. For example, 'She won't let me see the kids because she's nuts' may be reframed as 'What I hear from you is that you want to work out arrangements for the children to see each parent' and 'Well, he isn't coming to get the kids from my house because I don't want to see him ever because I hate his guts' may become 'What I hear from you is that you want to work out how changeovers can be less stressful'.

The mediator may then identify any common ground between you both. Unless that common ground is that you both hate each other.

Agenda setting

Work out what issues you want to try to resolve during the mediation and this could be things like 'When will our children, Jack and Jill, see each of us?', 'What school should they go to?' or 'How do we sell the house?', and 'When will they go up the hill?'. Each party is given a chance to choose the order of the agenda items.

Exploration

This is the scary part for mediators—where you let the parties talk to each other about the issues. In facilitative mediation the mediator acts as a referee by reminding parties not to talk over each other, stepping in to 'reframe' statements if they are getting too emotional, and reminding parties that they are there to try to resolve issues, not yell at each other.

It can be a difficult transition from lawyer to facilitative mediator, as the temptation is to jump in to give parties solutions. A good facilitative mediator will remember that the parties are there to work out their own solutions for their own children or property, not to have a solution imposed on them. As long as the discussion is not becoming abusive, it can be helpful for the parties to have their say in a safe environment. The mediator may have to again remind the parties about the agreed rules and reframe statements or bring parties back to the point. A mediator may say, 'I hear that you are very upset about this incident, but let's refocus back onto how to make things better in the future'.

The mediator might have private sessions with you both at this stage, to check in with you and to further explore the issues with you privately. The mediator won't (can't) tell your ex what you are saying in these sessions.

Options

The next step is to start to generate options; the mediator may help you both think about how options could practically work. (Apparently mediators are not allowed to say, 'That's the stupidest idea I have ever heard, are you actually serious?' Instead they have to say, 'So, how practically do you see that working in the future?')

Private session

The mediator may have a private session with you and a private session with your ex at this point. Again, to check in and to help work out if there are any stumbling blocks.

Negotiation

You and your ex now try to negotiate on the options you have come up with. The mediator's job is again to be the referee and to try to get you talking to each other rather than through the mediator.

Agreement ... or not

Many mediations are successful and result in an agreement. Family Relationship Centres can generally only draw up a parenting plan and you may both go and get legal advice at this point. It can be frustrating to have the other party go back on an agreement made in mediation but everyone has the right to get advice.

In a private mediation the mediator and lawyers may get together to formalise the agreement into a parenting plan, consent orders or a binding financial agreement (for property).

If you have agreed to split super (more on that later), you will need to first give the super fund a chance to suggest changes to the orders before you send them to court.

Evaluative mediation

In evaluative mediation, you have a mediator with a particular expertise who can not only facilitate the parties, negotiating, as with facilitative mediation, but may also give a view of each party's case. Using a former judge or a highly experienced lawyer as a mediator can be a good way to help parties come to an agreement together. Having someone experienced give you a reality check can be confronting but ultimately helpful. The mediator could remind you (and possibly your lawyer) of the high costs, delays and uncertainty of litigation.

Transformative mediation

In *The Promise of Mediation*, Robert A Baruch Bush and Joseph P Folger put forward the idea of transformative mediation, where the two main goals are to empower the disputing parties, and to enhance each party's recognition of the other.[68]

---

68 www.colorado.edu/conflict/transform/folger.htm.

Why would I use a private mediator when the public mediator is so much cheaper?

While there are sixty-five Family Relationship Centres currently open across Australia, including lots in rural and regional areas, you may not be able to find one that's convenient for you. Or, you may find the waiting lists are too long and you need your matter dealt with sooner than you can get in (some of the centres have very long waiting lists, and you may need an urgent mediation conference as a last-ditch effort to resolve an issue, such an agreement to take the children overseas for a family wedding).

Some people prefer to choose their own private mediator, who may specialise in things like very high-conflict divorces, or very high-value property pools (complete with lots of trusts, companies and self-managed super funds that may or may not be in a mess), or who have specialist backgrounds such as training in issues facing separating couples whose children have special needs.

Some mediators are psychologists rather than lawyers and this can be very helpful when conflict arises because of a teenager refusing to do what their parents want them to do (in other words, being a typical teenager) or because parents simply need assistance in working out what arrangements will suit a very young child, or a very upset child.

As mentioned, some mediators are experienced lawyers, former Family Court or Federal Circuit Court judges or court **registrars** and can provide an evaluative style of mediation, where the mediator provides their opinion on the competing proposals. This can be extremely helpful, as parties get a third, independent, opinion from a highly experienced professional. The mediator can challenge the parties and this can be very helpful as it is easy for parties (and their lawyers) to become entrenched in their positions, or to forget that while they may really be entitled to another $20 000, a fully litigated hearing may cost them $40 000.

Registrar—a court lawyer who can do things such as grant divorces, mediate at conciliation conferences, sign consent orders and decide the next step in a case.

You cannot have a lawyer attend a Family Relationship Centre mediation with you. In complex cases, it can be helpful to have your lawyer with you, which is why people with difficult matters often choose a private mediator.

Having your lawyer with you at mediation can be helpful, as the lawyer can provide advice regarding advantages and disadvantages of options put forward by the other party, and can help you formulate options yourself. The lawyer should be thoroughly prepared and usually a mediation position paper would be prepared and sent to the other side, and the mediator. The mediation position paper sets out what you want and why (using actual legal principles not just what Aunt Betty thinks because she watches *Judge Judy* a lot).

My ex refuses to go to mediation, or refuses to go to the mediator I suggested

It's pretty ironic when things are so far gone that you can't even get your ex to agree to the mediator. One man we know faced an almighty battle to get his soon-to-be-ex-wife to agree to go to mediation, and when he offered to pay as a way to help, she claimed that this was 'proof' of some kind of dastardly plot, and that he had chosen one of his mates as the mediator so as to trick her.

Mediation sounds all very well and good in principle but in practice, just the simple act of choosing a mediator can lead to horrible and stressful fights. It's funny (and not ha-ha) that you once decided together to get married, have babies and buy houses, and now you can't even agree on a mediator.

If you're going public, great—this is usually much easier (unless your ex thinks you've somehow gotten the federal government on board in your conspiracy against them). If you're using a private mediator, and your ex won't agree to them or is stonewalling (refusing to engage), then choose three that you'd be happy to go to, and ask your ex to make the final decision from those three. If they won't do that, ask them to put forward an alternative proposition within a specified timeframe (so, within three days). People who are being unreasonable find it quite difficult to continue to be unreasonable when they're given a choice of reasonable options.

I feel threatened by my ex and don't want to go to mediation

If you feel threatened, speak up. Tell the family dispute resolution provider, who will do an assessment at your private intake session of whether the matter is suitable for mediation, or suitable only with safety measures in place, such as having the parties in separate rooms with the mediator going between them (shuttle mediation).

If mediation fails, the next step can often be the commencement of a litigated matter. This means ... court.

Commencing legal proceedings

On average, about 5 per cent of all family breakdowns or disputes over things like relocation end up in the Federal Circuit Court or the Family Court. You end up in court when you can't agree on matters such as what arrangements will be made for your children, or how your property will be divided. The family courts have been starved of funding in recent years, and so very lengthy delays are not uncommon. It's quite usual for a matter to take between one to two years to be fully resolved.

As we've discussed, most matters go through the Federal Circuit Court. The Family Court is reserved for matters that are likely to be complex and need more than two days of trial, for international matters, and matters involving allegations of serious sexual or physical abuse (more on this below).

It usually comes as a surprise to find that you most likely will not have just one hearing, you may have a number of hearings before the trial or final hearing. After that there may be an appeal or proceedings about costs.

Usually after mediation, if matters have not settled, the following process will take place:

1. Notice of issues and future intentions

Either your lawyer or your ex's lawyer will send the other lawyer a written notice of issues and future intentions. This just really serves to get the ball rolling, and to start the process of going to court. A notice of issues and future intentions sets out what one side of the matter considers to be the things in dispute, and says what they are going to do about it (which is probably taking someone to court).

2. A reply to that written notice will be sent

This is pretty much the grown-up version of 'I know you are, but what am I?'

3. One of the sides will make an application to the court, which will be served on the other party

Once the application is filed with the court (either with the registry or online) it will show the case number and the date of the hearing. If the application is filed online, you can generally choose which date the first hearing will be on.

The application must be personally served on the other party, so this means that if they do not cooperate and there is a chance that they will not put in a response and turn up to the court date, the application must be served by a process server, which costs money.

The vast majority of matters are started in the Federal Circuit Court. Usually only the following matters are filed in the Family Court:

- international child abduction
- international relocation
- disputes about which country a matter should be heard in
- special medical procedures (such as gender reassignment and sterilisation)
- contravention and related applications in parenting cases, concerning orders that have been made in Family Court proceedings that have reached a final stage of hearing or a judicial determination and have been made within twelve months prior to filing
- serious allegations of sexual abuse of a child or serious family violence

- complex questions of jurisdiction or law
- matters where a trial will probably take more than four days of hearing time.[69]

The Magellan 'list' is a program for matters where there are serious allegations of physical and sexual child abuse.[70] In these matters there is a single judge who makes sure that the matter progresses and does not get bogged down and delayed.

This can include:

- early appointment of **an independent children's lawyer** and a family reporter
- establishing greater cooperation between the court, the independent children's lawyer and state-based child protection services, such as Child Safety Services in Queensland or Family and Community Services in New South Wales.

Independent children's lawyer—a lawyer appointed by the court, and usually paid for by Legal Aid, to represent a child's interests in a matter in the Federal Circuit Court or Family Court. The independent children's lawyer will meet with the child, if appropriate, and gather evidence by way of subpoenas, family reports and psychiatric assessments. The independent children's lawyer is a party to the matter. Legal Aid will seek a contribution to the costs of the independent children's lawyer from you if you have the means to pay.

4. A response to the application is filed with the court and served on the applicant

The **rules** of the court say that this should be done within fourteen days. Usually having the response within fourteen days doesn't

69 www.familycourt.gov.au/wps/wcm/connect/fcoaweb/about/policies-and-procedures/protocol-for-division-of-work-fcoa-fcc.

70 www.familycourt.gov.au/wps/wcm/connect/fcoaweb/family-law-matters/family-violence/child-abuse-allegations/child-abuse-allegations.

happen and sometimes we are lucky if we get the response the day of the first hearing.

> **Rules**—a set of directions that outlines court procedures and guidelines. The rules of the Family Court are the *Family Law Rules 2004* and the rules of the Federal Circuit Court are the *Federal Circuit Court Rules 2001*.

> **Applicant**—the person who applies to a court for orders (which means a decision is made and then turned into legally enforceable orders).

5. Opportunity to settle

Often, once the parties both file their material with the court, they realise that they are not really fighting over that much and suddenly the reality of having to pay their solicitors to go fight about not much hits home. Many matters settle here, either with consent orders emailed to the judge's chambers or handed up to the judge on the first hearing date. In family law, this is known as 'having an attack of the reasonables', and it's where many, many matters end.

Even if parties can't agree on final orders, they can sometimes agree on such orders as exchanging financial documents, going to mediation, having property valued and getting a report from a family consultant about what is in the children's best interests. Of course, this all should have been done in the pre-action procedure, but there is nothing like a court date to focus people's minds and make them suddenly decide not to fight to the death over two extra nights a month. Court is scary and stressful and it's all deeply unpleasant, and if it can be avoided, then it should be.

6. Mention or directions hearing (or possibly procedural hearing)

Usually there are a number of mentions (otherwise called directions hearings or procedural hearings) where parties let the judge know what is going on and whether any procedural orders need to be made. **Procedural orders** can include orders that a family report be prepared or a psychiatric assessment be done on one or all parties. There can be a lot of mentions and this gets expensive. In the Federal Circuit Court, mentions are usually on duty list days where a judge may hear thirty-plus matters, so the back of the courtroom will probably be packed.

> **Procedural order**—an order made by a court of a practical nature. For example, the court may order the parties to attend family dispute resolution.

7. Interim hearing

If the matter does not settle before court or on the first day of court, then depending on how many other matters are listed to be heard by your judge that day, and how urgent the issues raised by your case are, you may have an interim hearing. An interim hearing is not like **court hearings** that you see on TV, as usually parties do not give formal evidence, although the judge may wish to ask you questions. The judge may also wish to warn you about how expensive, time-consuming and horrible court is. (At this juncture feel free to roll your eyes and mutter, 'We get it!' under your breath—just don't do that to the judge. We know we've laboured the point on how horrible court is.)

> **Court hearing**—the date and time when a case is scheduled to come before the court.

Interim hearings can involve issues such as where a child will live until an actual trial, whether a family report should be obtained, whether a psychiatric assessment of one or both parties is necessary, whether one or both parties should submit to drug testing, whether a property should be sold or not, whether there are more financial disclosure documents to be exchanged and whether interim disbursements should be made.

Usually in interim hearings, witnesses do not get into the witness box and do not get cross-examined (put in the witness box and asked questions by the lawyers); rarely, the judge will ask for this to happen. The lawyers (or self-represented litigants) will make 'submissions', which are legal arguments to support their case, referring the judge to available evidence—for example, in affidavits or family reports. Since witnesses are not cross-examined, judges usually cannot make a decision about whether someone is lying or not—this is generally a matter for the trial (otherwise called a final hearing), where witnesses will be cross-examined at length.

Following on from the interim hearing, interim orders may be made on a variety of issues, such as to attend mediation, as to where the child will live, and any other issues that can't wait until the final hearing.

7. Further opportunity to settle

After the interim hearing, a matter may go back to mediation, or go to a first mediation, and parties will keep negotiating. Sometimes orders will be made that parties go off to parenting orders programs or joint post-separation counselling. These can be really helpful. Joint counselling in particular can be very useful in helping calm warring parents down and letting them explore issues that are preventing them from co-parenting. Exploring and trying to resolve issues with the help of a counsellor or psychologist can be preferable to having the issues ventilated in a court. There is nothing quite as humiliating as trying to explain to the other parent's barrister in front of a judge why you could not return uniforms or lunchboxes, or just had to send that nasty text.

One party or both parties may ask the court to issue **subpoenas** to third parties such as the police, doctors, psychologists or the ambulance service. These third parties then must give copies of notes, reports and the like to the court, and the parties (or more usually their solicitors) can read them in court. Usually they are either read by or provided to the family consultant.

Subpoena—a document issued by a court, at the request of a party, requiring a person to produce documents and/or give evidence to the court. You learn to spell it by spelling it out sub-po-ena but it's actually pronounced sah-*pee*-na.

8. Mention or a directions hearing

After the parties have had the chance to consider things like financial disclosure documents, material from third parties, reports from property valuers or family report writers and psychiatrists, the court may bring the matter back for a mention or directions hearing. Some judges like to do this a few times, just to give parties the opportunity to settle, or to make sure they really, *really* mean to go to trial.

9. Trial directions

After one more mention/directions hearing, the judge will then make trial directions and each judge seems to like different trial directions. Trial directions include filing and serving trial affidavits, which usually updates all of the previous affidavits. It can be tempting to have everyone who has ever met you do an affidavit saying what an all-round awesome person you truly are, but this is not a good idea and can lead to a judge either bumping the matter to the Family Court or making a costs order against you for bringing a bunch of irrelevant issues to court.

Going to trial

Okay, so you're going to court. You've done all you can within reason to settle, and you, or your ex, have determined that the only way forward is to go to court to ask the judge to resolve your issues for you. It's a pretty intimidating environment. Here's a heads-up on what to expect.

Who are all these people in court?

In the courtroom may be:

- your lawyer, who will tell you where to sit. Generally you will sit just behind your lawyer, who will be sitting at the 'bar table' (which is the long table in front of the judge's 'bench')
- your barrister, if you have one
- your ex's lawyer and/or barrister

- other litigants, their friends and family, and lawyers and barristers waiting for the next matter, who sit at the back of the court
- friends and family of yours and/or your ex may also sit at the back of the court, although if they are likely to be witnesses, they may be asked to leave
- law students who may be interning at the court
- the court reporter, who keeps a **transcript** of the court's proceedings (who said what)
- your ex
- the independent children's lawyer (ICL), if your child/ren has one, who sits in the middle of the 'bar table'
- child protection workers, if necessary
- the judge, or registrar (who may already be hearing another matter)
- the judge's associate (a lawyer who helps the judge run their matters and helps with writing the decision)
- the court support officer, who helps people appearing in the court
- the family report psychologist, who will have written the family report, if applicable
- the tipstaff, who helps support the administrative running of the court.

Transcript—a record of the spoken evidence in a court case, which the court reporter types up. All court hearings are recorded, except in uncontested divorce hearings. The court doesn't order transcripts in every case and doesn't provide transcripts to parties. If a party orders a transcript, they will have to pay for it themselves (unless and until you get costs awarded, yay).

What's the difference between a solicitor and a barrister?

About $5000 a day, mainly.

Just joking. Sort of.

A barrister is a specialist advocate who predominantly appears in court to argue cases on behalf of clients. They are 'instructed' (told all about the case) by solicitors. Barristers are experts in 'advocacy', which is getting up and arguing with each other in front of a judge.

Barristers refer to solicitors as 'book carriers' and solicitors refer to barristers as 'tossers'.[71]

What is the difference between a registrar and a judge?

About $300 000 a year in salary, mostly.

Not joking.

Registrars are 'court lawyers' and in the Family Court, they manage matters before they get to a judge. Things like case assessment conferences (the first major event in the Family Court in property cases), conciliation conferences (mediation) and procedural hearings are managed by registrars. Matters are handed over to the judges when they get more serious.

Conciliation conferences are mediations where a registrar from the Family Court or Federal Circuit Court is the mediator. Having an experienced court lawyer to facilitate negotiation and also offer an evaluation of the case is extremely valuable. The registrar can also make the orders if an agreement is reached (unless there is a superannuation interest to be split, as the super fund has to be given a chance to comment first—in this case a document called 'heads of agreement' can be drafted; these are basically orders that can be made once the super fund has its say).

71 That's only because we're jealous of their awesome wigs and gowns.

How much to go to court?

The fees payable in the Family Court or in the Federal Circuit Court are set by the federal government, and often change. By way of example, as at October 2017, the following fees were in place:[72]

Family Court

Application for consent orders	$160
Application for a decree as to nullity (divorce)	$1225
Reduced fee for divorce (available to low-income earners)	$410
Application for annulment of marriage	$1225
Initiating application (parenting orders or financial orders, final only)	$445
Notice of appeal to the full court (including from Federal Circuit Court)	$1305
Issue of subpoena	$55
Setting down for hearing fee	$825
Daily hearing fee	$825
Conciliation conference	$380

Federal Circuit Court

Application for divorce	$865
Application for divorce—reduced fee (available to low-income earners)*	$290
Initiating application (parenting orders or financial orders, final and interim only)	$330
Issue subpoena	$55
Setting down for hearing fee	$605
Daily hearing fee	$605
Conciliation conference	$380

* www.federalcircuitcourt.gov.au/wps/wcm/connect/fccweb/reports-and-publications/publications/family-law/guidelines-for-reduced-fee-divorce-and-decree-of-nullity-application.

72 Taken from www.familycourt.gov.au/wps/wcm/connect/fcoaweb/forms-and-fees/fees-and-costs/fees.

As you can see, the Federal Circuit Court is quite a bit cheaper than the Family Court, but it's still a very expensive process. These costs are on top of what you're paying your lawyer, but your lawyer will generally pay the court fees up front, and you will pay them back as 'disbursements' (money the lawyer has paid on your behalf that you owe), or your lawyer will pay them out of the trust account.

What do I need to be aware of in court?

Try to arrive at least half an hour before the time your matter is listed. Often it can be hard to find the hearing room and you want to give yourself plenty of time so you're not flustered. Your lawyer may also ask you to come earlier to have a conference about the case or to fill you in on any last-minute issues that your ex's lawyer (the other side) may have raised.

When you enter the court and it is already in session (when the judge is seated at the bench and the lawyers are talking or listening to the judge), you should briefly pause at the door and nod your head to the judge.

If you need to leave the courtroom and the court is in session, again pause briefly at the door, and nod to the judge as you leave. This is considered good courtroom etiquette and is how you show respect to the judge.

Do not have your mobile phone on in court, but if you must have it on, have it on mute and don't answer it in court under any circumstances. Being told off by the judge because your phone rings, or worse, because you answer it, is horrible.

If you are in the courtroom before the judge has entered, the judge's associate will announce the judge's entrance by saying, 'All rise'. At this point you must stand up, even if you are just sitting in the back of the courtroom. The judge will enter the room, and once he or she has sat down, you must also sit down. Don't sit down before the judge does. Each time the court adjourns, you must stand. The court officer will say, 'All rise' or 'Please stand'.

> **Adjourn**—change or postpone a court event (i.e. any time you or your lawyer has to go to court for your case) to another day or time.

Judges and barristers in the Family Court wear 'robes', which are long gowns. It might look silly but it serves an important function—it differentiates a judge from a normal person, and it's been shown that when judges and barristers aren't robed, there are significant increases in the rates of violent acts committed against them. In the Federal Circuit Court, judges are robed and barristers can choose to be robed or not.

You must also remove your hat (unless it is a religious head covering, which includes a colander if you are an adherent of the Church of the Flying Spaghetti Monster) and your sunglasses (including off the top of your head—unless you're Bono).

Can my children come to court with me?

No, unless they have been 'called' to give evidence. This almost never happens as children do not belong in court. If, in a very unusual case, a judge does want to talk to the children, this is done in the judge's chambers or with the family consultant.

Courts are very, very boring, and you must be quiet the vast majority of the time, and there will be lots of evidence being heard about sensitive matters. This is why it's not appropriate to bring your children. You must make other arrangements for their care, and be aware that even a brief 'mention', where your case is being 'mentioned' to the judge, can be delayed and delayed and it can take all day. There can also be a number of mentions, particularly if parties are waiting for things (such as a family report or counselling).

If a judge discovers that your children are sitting in the back of the courtroom, even if the children are not actually hearing solicitors tell the court how awful their parents are, you can expect the judge to be very unhappy and possibly draw some conclusions about your capacity to parent. The only exception to this is if you have a small baby and you're breastfeeding, in which case talk to your lawyer about how you should handle that issue.

Make sure your kids can be looked after from at least 8.30 a.m. to 5 p.m. (courts generally do not sit past 4.15 p.m., but sometimes they do and also your lawyer may wish to speak with you after the day's proceedings). Don't forget that you are probably going to be driving home in peak-hour traffic, so you may not make after-school care by 6 p.m.

What is an independent children's lawyer?

An independent children's lawyer (ICL) is a senior lawyer who is appointed by the court to represent your child's or children's best interests. A judge will make an order appointing an ICL after considering the matter, including the following factors:

- there are allegations of child abuse, whether physical, sexual or psychological
- there is an apparently intractable conflict between the parents
- the child is apparently alienated from one or both parents
- there are real issues relating to cultural or religious differences that affect the child
- whether the sexual preference of either or both of the parents or some other person having significant contact with the child is likely to impinge upon the child's welfare
- whether the conduct of either or both of the parents or some other person having significant contact with the child is likely to impinge upon the child's welfare
- there are issues of significant medical, psychiatric or psychological illness, including personality disorder, in relation to either party or a child or other persons having significant contact with the child
- based on the material filed by the parents, neither seems a suitable custodian

- a child of mature years (over about the age of twelve) is expressing strong views, giving effect to which would involve changing a long-standing custodial arrangement, or a complete denial of access to one parent
- one of the parties proposes that the child will be either permanently removed from the jurisdiction, or permanently removed to such a place within the jurisdiction as to greatly restrict, or for all practicable purposes exclude, the other party from the possibility of access to the child
- it is proposed to separate siblings
- none of the parties are legally represented and custody is at issue
- in applications to the court's welfare jurisdiction relating in particular to the medical treatment of the child's interests where they are not adequately represented by one of the parties.[73]

The ICL will gather evidence from reliable sources, including medical evidence relating to both the parents and the children. It can be very confronting for an ICL to be appointed to represent your children's best interests, because as parents we generally believe that we know what's best for our kids. It can be even more confronting when the ICL starts sending subpoenas off to your doctor, to hospitals, the police and your state's department of child safety, or when the ICL requests that you undergo a drug test.

However, the ICL offers you the gift of a third party making recommendations to the court when you are too close to the matter, or too upset, to think straight. An ICL also offers you a buffer between you and your ex, so the recommendations aren't coming from you. If your ex is especially incapable of being reasonable, they won't have just you to blame if things don't go 'their' way. They can blame the poor old ICL as well.

73 Re K (1994) 17 FAMLR 537.

Case study—Fred and Karen

Fred and Karen had two children, Bill and Ben. Fred and Karen separated after having had a stormy relationship marked by frequent arguments, domestic violence and drug abuse.

When they first split up, Fred kept the children and refused to let Karen see them, claiming that Karen was 'mental' and a 'druggie'. Karen made an urgent application to the court, and the judge ordered that an ICL be appointed. The judge also ordered that the ICL be able to request random urinalysis from the parties, and that the parties would have twenty-four hours to comply.

The judge also made an order that a family consultant provide an urgent report to the court.

When the ICL received the file, she asked the court to issue subpoenas to the police, to child safety, to the children's schools and to the local hospitals. She also requested that both parents submit to a urinalysis within twenty-four hours and provide the results as soon as they were available.

The material produced under subpoena showed that the police and child safety department had been pretty involved with the family, with quite a lot of notifications over the years, involving drugs, violence and verbal abuse. The children's school reports and attendances were dismal.

Karen's urinalysis results came back clear, but Fred's came back positive for methamphetamines. The family consultant recommended that the children live with Karen and spend time with Fred, supervised by Fred's mother for the interim.

The ICL suggested orders that ensured both Fred and Karen underwent counselling with their own counsellors and that the boys also saw their own counsellor.

Fortunately, all this was a wakeup call for both Karen and Fred, who both worked hard with their counsellors. After about a year of counselling and after both Karen and Fred returned three negative drug tests, the ICL agreed that the boys could spend unsupervised time with their dad.

What is a family report?

A family report is a report that either you, your ex, the judge hearing your matter, or the ICL appointed to represent your children will request. It is prepared by a registered, accredited psychologist or social worker, and includes information about your home life, your ex partner's home life, your children, you and your ex-partner, to help the court make a decision about your matter, on issues such as where the children will live and spend time with their parents.

The family report writer may interview you and your children separately, together, or both. They may speak with other people in your life, such as your new partner, your parents, or any other person they think plays a significant role in the lives of the child/ren. The report will be given to the court, the ICL (if there is one), you (or your lawyer if you have one) and your ex (or their lawyer if they have one).

You can't really 'prepare' for your meeting with the family reporter. Just tell the truth and remember to be child-focused (so, focused on what is best for your child, not on how much you hate your ex) at all times. The meeting with the family reporter is not your opportunity to tell them about how badly you've been treated by your ex, even if that's absolutely the case. Be the Sane Parent. Show that you can look to the future and that you can accept your children's other parent will be in that future in one way or another.

There are two sorts of family reports—a section 11F report or a section 62G report. (Oh, how lawyers love talking in code and TLAs—three letter acronyms.)

A section 11F report, or child inclusive memorandum, is a short memorandum prepared by a family consultant—a social worker or psychologist who works for or is engaged by the court. It is usually only about three pages long (but can be longer) and deals with immediate, urgent issues such as whether a parent poses an immediate threat to a child.

A section 62G report is a longer, more in-depth report that can go for about twenty to forty pages and can include details of interviews with both parents, new partners, grandparents, teachers, principals, joint counsellors, children's counsellors and doctors. It will also generally include interviews with older children and details of observations of the way that the children interact with parents, grandparents, step-parents and step-siblings.

Most report writers see you at their office, but some will see you at home, particularly if they wish to assess your home environment. There are a few things to be aware of:

- Everything you say can be used in the report—there are no 'off-the-record' conversations.
- Everything you do can be used in the report—right up to the rude gesture you made to your ex in the waiting room (or the rude gesture they made to you).
- Report writers can be very literal people, so if you say sarcastically, 'Yeah, sure I hit my kids, all the time', that can translate into the report as 'Mother admitted to hitting her kids all the time'. If you say, in a moment of anger, 'Well, why doesn't she just have them all the time then?', this can translate into 'Father made a proposal that the children live with the mother'. You must try to be as careful and precise in the language you use as possible.
- Report writers aren't on 'your side'. You must remain calm and collected and child-focused at all times and resist the urge to use them as a counselling service. We have had many clients who have reported to us that the report writer was 'really friendly' and 'seemed to totally get where I was coming from' only for the report to come out saying that our client was manipulative and not child-focused.
- If you are making allegations of abuse against your child's other parent, it is imperative that you are absolutely truthful, for the sake of your child. Don't embellish. The smallest

embellishment will be used against you. If you don't know the answer to a question, don't try to come up with one. Simply say, 'I don't know'. It is crucial that you remain child-focused at all times and that you don't come across as simply trying to reduce your child's time with their other parent because you don't like them.

What do I wear to court or to family report interviews?

It's very important that you turn up to court looking respectable and professional. There are no 'rules' as such, which can be confusing, and the Family Court (un)helpfully states 'court is a formal place and you should dress accordingly'. Which really clears that up.

So here's our take on it. Men should wear:

- long dress pants (not jeans)
- lace-up shoes with socks
- a button-up shirt, preferably with a tie
- a belt
- a jacket.

Women should wear:

- a skirt and blouse in muted colours (yes, we know, a *blouse*); or long pants and blouse, again preferably in muted colours such as black, white or grey
- a jacket (optional)
- neat, conservative closed shoes (such as court shoes)
- hair done neatly, such as in a ponytail or brushed away form the face.

Do not:

- have very visible tattoos on show
- wear high-vis gear

- wear very bold, bright colours (we once had a client turn up to a hearing in head-to-toe neon fuchsia—hat, gloves, suit, heels, handbag, lipstick and nails)
- wear clothes showing a lot of skin (leave the plunging necklines, thigh-high slits or mesh panels for a decent evening out)
- wear skyscraper heels, not least because you are probably going to be on your feet for a lot of the day as you wait
- wear clothes with obscenities printed on them (you'd be surprised—we once had a client show up to his DUI with 'F**K THE POLICE' written on his t-shirt, only it was written without the stars)
- wear ripped clothes, especially with the logos of alcoholic drinks on them when you are facing allegations of being an alcoholic (and again, you would be surprised)
- wear sunglasses on your head or your motorcycle helmet into the courthouse
- forget to wear shoes, even if you are a hippy and think that shoes stop your connection to the earth's vibrations, or something.

You may think 'I'll turn up however I please', and absolutely, you can. But if you want to get the best result for *you*, then dress neatly and professionally. It's a courthouse, with a judge, and they are often very conservative people. By dressing neatly, and appropriately, you'll give yourself the advantage of not letting anyone literally judge you on how you look.

Being cross-examined by your ex in court

It can be very distressing if your ex is self-representing and therefore has the opportunity to cross-examine you in court. If you're in this situation, you should be aware that your lawyer will object, should the questioning be irrelevant or badgering. The judge can also step in and allow you to refuse to answer questions that are unnecessarily distressing. In such situations, however, you are really dependent on your lawyer or the judge to, in fact, step in.

Your lawyer may not object if they feel that the questioning is actually helpful to your case. The judge will be making their decision based on all of the evidence, including how you both look and what you both ask each other, or have your lawyers ask each other, when you are in the witness box.

Sometimes, your ex is your best witness. In one protection order matter, a client's ex continually made faces at her when she was giving evidence. He also, charmingly, pushed his chair out as far as he could when she was walking to the witness box, meaning she had to pretty much climb over his knees. The magistrate saw all of this and was scathing in their judgment.

Under recent changes made to the Act, if you are a victim of domestic violence (even if it is thus far unproven), you will not be subjected to cross-examination by the alleged perpetrator. However, this is cold comfort to those who are not in that category, and still have to face their ex staring them down from the witness box.

How is a decision made?

After hearing all the evidence and considering the reports of any experts, the judge will reserve their decision. The written part of a decision, where the judge writes up the reasons for it and the orders they are making, can take some time. Orders come after the decision has been made. Sometimes this takes weeks, sometimes it is months. That's why it's so important to try to ensure that any interim decisions (formal or otherwise) are something that you can live with, because they will be in place for some time.

And if you or your ex don't agree with the decision of the judge because you think they have made a mistake in law or in fact, you can **appeal** the decision to a higher court. This is not a chance to argue your case again.

Appeal—a procedure that allows a party to challenge the decision made by a court, in a higher court. It takes a long time and costs a lot of money to appeal a decision. There is also a risk that a party will have to pay the costs of the other party if an appeal is unsuccessful.

For appeals from a decision of a judge of the Federal Circuit Court, once the appeal is filed the chief justice of the Family Court makes a decision about whether the appeal will be heard by a single judge or three judges. For the Family Court of Australia, you appeal to the Full Bench of the Family Court of Australia. The next court of appeal is the High Court.

An appeal doesn't mean you don't have to comply with the order that was made in the decision you're appealing. You still have to comply, unless new orders are made, either after the appeal is heard or the previous orders being stayed until the appeal is heard.

I spend all my time in my lawyer's office crying—how can I stop?

Don't worry too much about this. Family lawyers are used to clients crying. It's an occupational hazard and we have boxes of tissues everywhere. You're talking about the division of your property and the custody of your children—we expect you to be a bit emotional.

However, you also don't want to waste your time and money crying. A good way to get through it is to have a clear idea of what you want to discuss. This is where the worksheet that goes along with this chapter, and the one in the previous chapter, can come in handy. If you have a structured plan of what you want to talk about, this can allow you to concentrate on what's important.

We know it's an ordeal, and we're sorry you're going through it.

WORKSHEET 5
QUESTIONS FOR MY LAWYER ABOUT ARRANGEMENTS FOR OUR CHILDREN

This worksheet is an opportunity for you to jot down any questions you have for your lawyer before you go into the meeting or teleconference, and a space for you to make notes of the answers. This can be helpful if you are quite upset, or if you're stressed at the time of the meeting, because you can easily go back over your notes afterwards. It's totally normal to find these discussions extremely upsetting, and very often people cry, a lot. Don't worry about it, we're totally used to it (we'll just charge you for the tissues).

Date:	**Date:**
Questions for my lawyer about arrangements for our children	**Answers**
1.	
2.	
3.	
4.	
5.	
6.	
7.	
8.	
9.	
10.	

7

Child support

The only thing separated parents uniformly agree on is that the child support system in Australia is unfair. It can be a major source of ongoing conflict between separated parents.

The child support section on the website for the Department of Human Services (DHS) can be found at www.humanservices.gov.au/customer/dhs/child-support. You can both make a claim for child support and pay your child support online.

Child support is calculated according to the number of nights of care each parent has, the number of children the couple has, any other children the paying parent has, the age of the children, and the incomes of both parents.

The DHS has an online child support calculator, which we discussed previously, and can be found here: www.processing.csa.gov.au/estimator/About.aspx.

There are three ways to pay or be paid child support—through a private collection agreement, via self-management, or through the DHS, which is run by the federal government.

Self-management

Collecting via a self-management agreement can work well if you have a cooperative relationship. Some paying parents much prefer self-management, because it means the payroll officer at their workplace doesn't have access to intimate details of their life, which is fair enough, and it means that a mutual decision can be made for the benefit of your family, not according to some calculator.

Neither party has to register with the DHS. Self-management means the amount to be paid and the way in which the money is to be paid are managed between the parents. You can pay and be paid as much or as little as you both decide upon. It could mean, for example, that one parent pays the school fees and the other parent the medical expenses.

You can't choose self-management if you receive more than the base rate of the family tax benefit. Unless you have registered with the DHS, unpaid amounts can't be collected by child support, although you can change to private collection or collection through the DHS at any time.

Do use self-management if you're a billionaire, but *don't use* self-management if you find it hard to stand up to your ex or if there's a power imbalance between you. At the very least, make sure you do the child support estimate. Just be aware that threats to cut off child support, or to stop paying school fees, or to take you to court for sole custody if you don't agree to this, that or the other are not uncommon with self-managment, can be effective control mechanisms, and are also, frankly, economic abuse.

Private collection

This is where the parent who is paying the child support does so based on a child support assessment agreement or a court order (yes, the courts can order child support payments in 'special circumstances', such as when one of you is a millionaire and the other is a stay-at-home parent). In this option, there's little other interaction with the DHS, unless the paying parent doesn't cough up the cash.

Do use private collection if you're on speaking terms with one another and have a pretty mature approach to finances and a good understanding of what raising kids costs, but *don't use* private collection if you can't discuss financial matters without it degenerating into a shouting match that can be heard from space.

Collection via the Department of Human Services

This is where the government agency in charge of child support collections both assesses and collects (or, really, passes on) the child support money from the payer to the payee. The DHS can also get 'garnishee orders' whereby if there's a history of non-payment, child support is taken directly from the wages and/or tax return of the paying parent and paid to the receiving parent. Some people underreport their income in order to avoid their child support responsibilities, which is a crappy thing to do, because the people who really lose are the children. There are very few single parents living the high life on their child support payments, after all.

Do use the DHS to collect if you and your ex hate each other with the burning intensity of a thousand suns, but *don't use* the DHS to collect if you've already got a standover man doing it for you. There's no need to be greedy. Just kidding, we don't condone standover men (plus we hear they are quite expensive).

Generally speaking, if the parents have equal time with the children, child support may not be payable unless there is a disparity in income, but all child-related expenses (such as medical, child care or after-school care) should be split down the middle. Anyone who thinks that child support actually pays half the expenses of raising kids is deluding themselves. Getting out of paying child support is probably the worst of all possible reasons for trying to get equal parenting time and almost always ends in tears.

Payment to third parties

If you have less than 14 per cent of care, you can ask the DHS to accept that payment to third parties is the equivalent of paying child support. The payments have to actually relate to the care of the children, and the most common are school fees or payments to the mortgage over the home the children are living in.

Child support special assessment

Sometimes the usual formula is not appropriate for a family situation, and an application can be made to change the child support assessment in special circumstances. It's not at all funny or immature that lawyers often refer to child support Special Assessment Applications as Spec Ass Apps.

The form is available on the Human Services website.[74] For each category, the child support officer making the decision must work out if it will be just and equitable for you, your ex and your child or children, and must consider factors such as the nature of the duty to maintain a child, the needs of the child, the income, earning capacity, property and financial resources of the child and the parties, the commitments of the parties to support themselves or other children or people, and any hardship caused to the child, the payer, the payee and any other child or person the payer or payee has a duty to support.

The reasons for changing a child support assessment in special circumstances are set out on the form, with examples:

Reason 1	**The costs of spending time with or communicating with the children are more than 5 per cent of your adjusted taxable income amount (this includes your child care bill, if that bill is more than 5 per cent of your income).**	This can be a bit of a kick in the guts for a parent who is literally left holding the baby—the other parent gets to ask the DHS to reduce their payments because they moved away and spending time with the kids suddenly costs more. All of the circumstances will be taken into account, though, including any hardship it may cause to the payer, the payee and the child.
Reason 2	**The child(ren) has special needs.**	An assessment can be changed if one parent has a lot of out-of-pocket costs for the child or children (after rebates and NDIS), such as orthodontic work, medication and medical expenses.

74 www.humanservices.gov.au/sites/default/files/documents/cs1970-1512en.pdf.

Reason 3	**There are extra costs in caring for, educating or training the child(ren) in the way both parents intended.**	This is the school fee ground, although it is also commonly used for nanny-related expenses. If you and your ex agreed that the children go to a private school and/or have a private nanny and your ex refuses to contribute towards the fees, then you can ask that the child support formula be changed to include these fees. Factors such as the earning capacity and commitments of both parents are taken into account. So if you are earning $50 000 a year and your ex is earning $350 000 and your ex is demanding that you pay half of the school fees as well as your mortgage, the disparity of income will be taken into account.
Reason 4	**The child(ren) has income, an earning capacity, property and/or financial resources.**	If a child is working full time and meeting many of their own expenses, then this may be taken into account. So if your seventeen year old is earning a full-time wage, this can be factored into the assessment. Or perhaps your seven-year-old is a YouTube star and their channel makes more in one day than you do in a month.
Reason 5	**You have provided money, goods or property for the benefit of the child(ren).**	If you are paying the mortgage on the house that your ex and the children are living in, and you have not been ordered to do this, then that can be taken into account in a change of assessment.
Reason 6	**The costs of child care for child(ren) under twelve years of age are more than 5 per cent of your adjusted taxable income amount.**	Child care is incredibly expensive and if it reaches more than 5 per cent of your taxable income, then this should be taken into account.
Reason 7	**You have out-of-the-ordinary necessary expenses to support yourself.**	These have to be reasonable. You cannot claim that your loan on your superyacht or Lamborghini prevents you from paying child support. High medical costs for yourself can be taken into account.

Reason 8	**Your ex is earning more or is able to earn more, or they have resources such as super that they can draw on.**	If your ex seems to be earning a lot more than their taxable income, especially if they are self-employed or own a company, or earn Defence Reserve pay (this does not get included in taxable income), then the child support officer can go through bank statements, and talk to accountants and other third parties. The sorts of things that business owners do to make their tax affairs efficient (perfectly legally) can simply be ignored by the child support officer, who can just deem that you or your ex is earning more. If your ex lets the DHS know that they are now not earning an income, but you are aware that they have received a redundancy, you can ask for a special assessment under this ground. A redundancy will be picked up in your ex's next tax return, but this is cold comfort to a parent receiving no child support for up to a year. If your ex has retired and tells the DHS that they are no longer receiving an income, you can ask the child support officer to take into account that multimillion-dollar super they now have access to.
Reason 9	**You have a duty to support another person.**	If your spouse or child from another relationship has medical needs, you can ask the child support officer to take these into account.
Reason 10	**You have a responsibility to support a resident child.**	If you are supporting a stepchild who lives with you most of the time, has lived with you for two continuous years and the child's biological parents are unable to support them, then you can ask the DHS to take this into account. Any decision still has to take into account any hardship caused to your ex and your biological children.

8

Special days

Although special days and celebrations are really part of parenting negotiations, they can cause so many issues that we have given the topic its very own chapter.

When you're a newly separated person, the first Christmas or Eid or Hanukkah or Diwali can really take on a massively outsized significance, and can lead to enormous conflict between you and your ex. And boy, don't those fights roll around quickly.

For most if not all family lawyers, the busiest season is September through to February, and that's mainly due to people fighting about Christmas plans when they're separated, or they're separating post-Christmas after yet another hideous holiday season. In fact, Rebekah has been a real pain about writing her share of this book because it's October.

There are a few different ways to organise Christmas Day, and again it will largely depend on your kids' ages. You will have considered this in your parenting plan or your consent orders, but disputes about Christmas are, again, why the last three months of the year are money-making gold for family lawyers.

A year-about split schedule works like this:

Year one (say, even-numbered years)	The kids are with parent 1 from midday Christmas Eve to midday Christmas Day, and with parent 2 from midday Christmas Day to midday Boxing Day.
Year two (say, odd-numbered years)	The kids will be with parent 2 from midday Christmas Eve to midday Christmas Day, and with parent 1 from midday Christmas Day to midday Boxing Day.

These arrangements apply regardless of which parent the children are spending time with immediately before Christmas Eve. It's definitely a bit awful waking up on Christmas morning without your kids (our tip—sleep in as late as you possibly can and don't go on social media, where every update will be pictures of smiling, happy families sharing in the Christmas spirit), but it's very exciting when they get home at midday. With this schedule, every second year you can plan a big Christmas Eve party, and every other year you can have a lovely Christmas lunch with your children.

The downside is, of course, that you can't ever really go away over the Christmas break. If you've always wanted a white Christmas and you live in the tropics, you'll never get to have that—not until the kids are older, anyway. Also, after spending time with both families at Christmas, the children are usually feral, sugar-fuelled nuclear bombs by about 6 p.m. If they are going to their other parent at midday, it can be tempting to give them more red cordial and a set of the cheap crayons that don't wash off walls just before they go, but this would be *very bad parenting*.

Splitting Christmas means that the kids get to spend time with both their parents and families on Christmas Day, and that's really important. Other families swap Christmas Day and Boxing Day year on, year off, and often find that works well, too, although the downside is that the kids can't see both their parents on Christmas Day. It does mean that no one is necessarily travelling on Christmas Day, though, and if you have family who live more than an hour away, with this schedule you can see them on Christmas Day as well, instead of being tied down to a strict deadline to either pick up or drop off your kids on the day.

An important consideration here is talking through with your kids (if they're old enough—say, over ten or eleven) what they would prefer.

Playing happy families at Christmas—give it time

The good news is that even the most hideous, angry divorces can ultimately turn into functional friendships or at least cooperative co-parenting relationships, given the passage of time and the ceasing of jerk-like behaviours, and family functions (such as shared Christmases that don't require military-level planning skills) can once again be held with both of the former spouses present.

But that's not going to happen overnight.

One woman we know was faced with infidelity during a very long (thirty-five-year) marriage and her husband ultimately left and married his affair partner. After some time had passed (ten-plus years) it was possible for the former couple to come together as friends at major family functions (such as birthdays, baptisms, weddings, funerals) without any antipathy or anger. The trick here is to give it time—it really does heal (most) wounds.

As tempting as it is to try to normalise matters as quickly as possible, if you've left a marriage, give your former spouse time to recover. It's not fair to rush them into a new, non-romantic relationship with you when you've devastated all their hopes and dreams for their future.

It may take a lot more time than you think. Don't force your former spouse into accepting your new spouse into their life—it's disrespectful and unfair, and it's not going to work. You might want to play happy families and absolve yourself of guilt over the pain you've caused, but it doesn't work that way.

If you've been left, don't feel you have to accept anything you're not comfortable with. You don't have to agree to shared family Christmases for 'the sake of the children' or having your ex and their new partner at your kids' birthday parties if you're not up to it. In fact, Rebekah would prefer that you didn't agree to it, as she has dealt with more than one client being arrested on Christmas Day after an all-in brawl kicked off—family lawyers deserve time off for Christmas Day too.

Don't feel bad about not being ready to share these special days. The time will probably come when you can easily (if not happily) be in the company of your ex, but for most people that's a good five or ten years down the track, especially if the split was very acrimonious.

Case study—Stephanie and Peter

Stephanie and Peter separated after four years of marriage. They had one child together, Penny, who was three, and Peter had two children from his previous marriage—Anna (seven) and George (nine), whom he had shared custody of. Stephanie felt that since Peter already had Anna and George for half of Christmas Day, Penny should spend the whole day with her, and spend Boxing Day with Peter. She didn't want to be by herself for any part of Christmas Day.

Peter felt that Penny should be able to spend time with her siblings on Christmas Day, and that he should be able to spend time with Penny as well. He preferred a year-about split Christmas Day, which is what he had with Anna and George.

Stephanie refused to compromise and the matter eventually went to the Family Court for a decision. The court ordered that Penny spend Christmases in odd-numbered years with Stephanie, and Christmases in even-numbered years with Peter.

This was not the outcome Stephanie expected, despite her legal advice to the contrary, and she was very upset. She thought that she would be able to get a year-about split if she didn't get the whole day. Peter was angry that the matter had had to go to court, and refused to then compromise on the split day.

The legal costs for both parties were in excess of $40 000.

While Stephanie and Peter's situation is a common one, and one that all family lawyers have dealt with, there can also be times when, after some time has passed, parents can come together without acrimony, and sometimes even as friends.

Case study—John and Ellie

John and Ellie divorced twelve years ago, after nineteen years of marriage. They had two children, Mark and David. Mark and David were now both married, and between them had five children. A few months before Christmas, Mark sent both John and Ellie a text message asking them to his house for Christmas lunch with David and all the children.

John had had an affair at the end of the marriage, and had married his affair partner, but that relationship had since ended. Both John and Ellie were very worried about how the lunch would go, as they had seldom seen each other in the intervening years. To their surprise, Christmas lunch was wonderful, and they both had a lovely day playing with their grandchildren and reminiscing about their own children's Christmases.

John found that he really liked Ellie's husband, Michael, and he was very glad to see Ellie so happy, as he had always thought of her as one of his best friends during their marriage. Ellie felt as though an enormous weight had been lifted from her shoulders and she was very glad that her relationship with John had been normalised. She had missed his friendship and was very glad to have the opportunity to create a new grandparenting relationship with him.

Birthdays, Mother's Day, Father's Day, Grandparent's Day and other special days

Make sure you include arrangements for birthdays and other special days in your parenting plans or consent orders. We spoke briefly about this in Chapter 6. Children want to spend time on their birthdays with both their parents, and you will naturally wish to spend time with your child as well.

The Act specifies that substantial and significant care means that the time the child spends with the parent allows:

- the child to be involved in occasions and events that are of special significance to the parent

- the parent to be involved in the child's daily routine; and occasions and events that are of particular significance to the child.

If you're not at the point where you can amicably go out for dinner with your ex and your child on your child's birthday, then your orders or plan can include provisions whereby the parent who did not spend time with the child on the morning of their birthday can spend time with them in the afternoon. For example, you could pick them up from school and go out for afternoon tea, or an early dinner. However, if taking your child out for dinner on their birthday is important to you and your ex, it's only fair that you alternate years so you both have the opportunity to do so.

It's also important to have a plan for birthday parties. It's pretty dysfunctional to have two separate birthday parties each year for your child with the same kids invited, and, frankly, it makes you fodder for school-gate gossip among the parents. You don't want your kid to be put in the position where everyone knows their family is dysfunctional. No one wants to buy two presents or go to two parties for the one kid, and you can be sure that the other parents will whinge about it, probably within earshot of their children, who will repeat it back verbatim to your child, their teacher, the school custodian and the vice-principal.

A good approach here is to agree that parent 1 will hold parties in even-numbered years and parent 2 will hold parties in odd-numbered years. The best approach, of course, is to get to the point where you can amicably both host your child's birthday party together without NATO having to negotiate the terms, but that day may be some time off, or may never come.

For days like Mother's Day and Father's Day, make sure your orders or plan allows for your kids to be dropped off the day before so that you can spend time with them. There's nothing sadder than mooching around by yourself when everyone else is enjoying the day with their kids.

If you alternate weekends with the kids, then it may just be easier to have orders that allow for alternate weekends taking into account

Mother's Day and Father's Day. It will all equal out in the wash, especially if the orders will be in place for a good decade.

If, however, your ex is the same sex as you, you will have to ensure that your orders include a split Mother's or Father's Day, or alternate years (so the kids are with parent 1 in even-numbered years and parent 2 in odd-numbered years), so that you can both have the opportunity to celebrate that day with your kids.

Some families have to also make arrangements as to which grandparent is allowed to turn up to their grandchild's school Grandparent's Day. We have seen many cases where things have gone badly wrong at such events. If the grandparents cannot get along, then a year-about schedule is generally the fairest option. The worst outcome would be for the child to feel anxious or worried because both (or all) grandparents turn up and fight with one another, or, even worse, are cold and silent. It's hardly the point of Grandparent's Day, is it?

9

Your property settlement

Now that you've sorted out your children, if you have them, it's time to talk about property. Oftentimes child and property matters are negotiated at the same time, especially if you've managed to mediate your outcome, but sometimes finalising your property settlement is a major sticking point and can take years to resolve.

Property settlements, especially those including the transfer of shares, investment property, companies or assets from a company, can have serious taxation implications and you should discuss these with your lawyer and your accountant.

De facto threshold

The Family Law Act says that the court can make a property order in de facto matters only if:

- the length of the relationship is **two years**; or
- there is a child of the relationship; or
- the applicant made 'substantial contributions' and it would be an injustice if the court did not make an order; or
- the relationship was registered under a law (civil union).

'Substantial contributions' would be:

- financial contributions to the acquisition, conservation or improvement of property—so, actually putting money into your property
- non-financial contributions to the acquisition, conservation or improvement of property—so, something like significant renovations or building, or working in a family business (i.e. doing the books) or on a family farm for no pay for years
- welfare contributions—caring for a child or doing the majority of the housework.

Time limits

Don't forget the time limits! They have a tendency to sneak up and catch people out.

- For married people, the time limit is twelve months after the date that a divorce order takes effect or decree of nullity is made, although consent orders can be made out of time without the court first giving leave.
- For de facto partners, the time limit is two years after separation, although consent orders can now be made out of time without the court first giving leave.

If you miss these time limits, unless both parties agree, you need the leave of the court to proceed and the judge may not necessarily give you this leave.

What is a property settlement?

A property and financial settlement is an agreement reached between you and your former spouse, or one imposed on you by the court, relating to the division of the assets held by one or both parties to the marriage, including:

- superannuation (this is a major source of conflict—many people can't *believe* they have to split their super)

- property (including any investments and the marital home, and property owned before marriage)
- business interests
- stocks
- bonds
- inheritances
- savings
- household goods, including artworks
- cars and boats
- personal effects, such as jewellery.

Liabilities of the marriage, such as credit card debts, mortgages, and other debts such as personal loans, will also be taken into consideration. It doesn't matter if property is held in just one spouse's name or not—it all goes into the asset pool for divvying up. There's also no rule that says the assets and liabilities must be divided fifty-fifty—there's a complex formula that we'll go into more detail about later.

You don't need to wait to finalise your divorce before you start your property settlement—you can get it underway as soon as you separate, if you want. Bear in mind that assets are valued as at the date of any order/trial/mediation, so the sooner you have things sorted out, the sooner you can both financially move on.

The family law courts have had power to make orders about superannuation since 28 December 2002; before, superannuation was treated as a financial resource. Back in those days it was not uncommon for the husband to have a lot of super and the wife to have very little super, so the wife would receive all or most of the assets because the husband was going to retire comfortably with his super. The government recognised that this was not a great way to organise finances for either party, so super splitting was brought in. You can also have flagging orders but these are rare. A flagging order is where the court orders that no action is to be taken in relation to splitting the super until the value of the super account is settled. Once the order is lifted, the super can then be split.

> **Super split**—where super is 'split' from one party's super account and put into the other party's super account, either by a superannuation agreement (usually contained in a binding financial agreement) or by court order.

Some schemes, such as the Defence Force Retirement and Death Benefits Scheme (DFRDB), can be tricky to deal with. Some or all of the DFRDB is generally paid as a guaranteed income for life, rather than as a lump sum, so you should seek advice.

How do I finalise my property settlement?

A property settlement can be finalised a few different ways.

By agreement

You and your former spouse can agree to divide your assets and liabilities without any outside interference. This is often an option where there are very few assets and even fewer liabilities. For example, if you both have roughly the same amount of superannuation, have no children, have only been married for a few years, earn the same amount of money, and are currently renting, you may just decide to divide up the savings account and go your separate ways. The risk here, of course, is that there's nothing to stop your former spouse from coming after you for more money down the track. An agreement between the two of you isn't legally binding and you will not be able to transfer assets without paying stamp duty.

If you have a lot of assets, and you and/or your spouse earn high incomes (known as a high-value divorce), you must seek legal advice. Don't just believe your ex when they say they've worked out a fair and reasonable settlement. We know of many cases where one partner has been told that they're getting a fair deal, when in fact they were entitled to much, much more.

By binding financial agreement

A binding financial agreement (BFA) is a written agreement reached by consent, usually negotiated by your lawyers, that finalises your property settlement without having to go to court. You both have to have independent legal advice and a certificate from an Australian legal practitioner saying you've been legally advised on the effect of the agreement on your rights and on the advantages and disadvantages to you at the time of signing. The court does not consider the BFA unless one of the parties requests that it be set aside, and there's no requirement that it be 'just and equitable'—that is, a fair deal for both of you.

If a BFA meets all of the criteria set out in the Family Law Act regarding independent legal advice and the court does not find that it should be set aside because of, for example, fraud, misrepresentation or a person trying to use the BFA to defraud a creditor by putting everything into their spouse's name, the court will usually follow it—so it is actually binding. The BFA has to be done properly, however, and according to the Act, or a court can find that it is not binding and so can set it aside.

Reputable lawyers will refuse to give advice on a BFA if there is any sign of duress or fear from either of the parties. If you want a BFA a week before your wedding, or settlement of a house purchase, it is likely that your lawyer will say, 'No way' when asked to give advice. In late 2017 the High Court considered a case where a BFA was signed four days before a wedding. The parents and sister of the bride-to-be had flown to Australia from overseas, guests had been invited, the dress had been made and the reception booked. A further, similar BFA was signed just after the wedding. The parties later separated and the wife asked the Federal Circuit Court to overturn the agreements. The matter went on appeal to the Family Court and then to the High Court, which held that the husband took advantage of the wife's vulnerability to obtain the agreements, which were entirely inappropriate and wholly inadequate. Although the husband had died by the time the matter was heard in the High Court, the outcome was that the agreements were overturned and the wife's claim for property settlement would be heard in the Federal Circuit Court at a later date.[75]

This is because it is pretty well established that weddings and purchasing houses are expensive and stressful events, and being jilted at the altar, possibly being left without a home and maybe with visa issues (and potentially being sued in the process) is a huge fear for some people.

In one case, the judge, not surprisingly, found that the husband threatening the wife with prosecution for forgery if she did not sign a BFA was duress and set the BFA aside.[76]

By consent orders

Consent orders are drafted by you, or your lawyer, or your ex or their lawyer, and they must be submitted to the court for consideration. A registrar (again, an experienced lawyer employed by the court) will consider whether the parenting arrangements are in the best interests of the children and whether the effect of the property orders is *just and equitable* in all the circumstances.

If they fail either of these, then the registrar can reject them or ask that parties give an explanation of how on earth they think their proposal is in any way just and equitable or in the best interests of the children.

Consent orders can include your parenting arrangements and your financial arrangements in the one document—they do not need to be separate. So, you can have one application for consent orders for both issues.

By orders of the court

If you cannot reach a mutual agreement as to the finalisation of your property agreement, you can apply to the court to make one for you. You don't have to get your ex to agree to this—you can just make the application.

75 http://eresources.hcourt.gov.au/downloadPdf/2017/HCA/49)
76 Tsarouhi v. Tsarouhi [2009] FMCAfam 126.

In Chapter 6, we discussed what happens when you commence legal proceedings, and what happens when you actually go to court. The procedure is pretty much the same for property matters.

Although an application to the court should be a last resort, it can be necessary if negotiation is dragging on, one party is stalling or it is becoming a huge source of stress for you—this is a hard thing to agree on! If a party seems to have disappeared all the assets or is threatening to disappear all the assets, then court is sometimes necessary.

Your lawyer (or you, if you're self-representing) will firstly decide which court to file in—the Family Court or the Federal Circuit Court. The Family Court can hear matters that contain certain, more serious, issues, if the hearing will take longer than four days of hearing time. Otherwise, your matter will most likely be heard in the Federal Circuit Court.

As when making a decision about whether to make consent orders or not, the court has to make a decision that is just and equitable in all the circumstances and the same factors will apply. For considerations involving the kids, again refer back to Chapter 6.

What property orders can a court make?

The court can make orders declaring that a party owns property, for the alteration of property interests,[77] and injunctions to protect persons or property.[78]

The power to adjust property interests is pretty far reaching and can include making an order that a home be transferred to either party or a child to the marriage, or that money be paid to either party or to the child of a marriage. The court also has power to order that a party's property vesting in a bankruptcy trustee be transferred to the non-bankrupt spouse or to a child of the marriage, or that a bankruptcy trustee pay money to the non-bankrupt spouse or to a child of the marriage.

77 Section 79 *Family Law Act 1975*.
78 Section 114 *Family Law Act 1975*.

What does the court have to consider when making property orders?

Before making orders altering property interests, the court has to firstly consider whether it is 'just and equitable' to even make orders. Then the court has to consider:

- What the net property pool is (that is, all the assets and liabilities must be considered, no matter when they were acquired—even post-separation assets).
- Who made what contribution to the property pool (financial contributions like income and inheritances, non-financial contributions like renovations or working for free in the family business and welfare contributions as the primary homemaker or parent) before, during and after the relationship.
- What each party's future needs are (including the age, state of health, income, property, earning capacity, commitments necessary to support themselves or children or other dependents; the extent to which the party whose maintenance is under consideration has contributed to the income, earning capacity, property and financial resources of the other party; the duration of the marriage and extent to which it has affected either party's earning capacity; the financial circumstances of any repartnering).[79]
- Whether the effect of the orders is just and equitable in all the circumstances, including if the orders have an effect on the earning capacity of a party (especially in matters involving the family farm or business).

Duty of disclosure

Each party to a property settlement matter has a duty to make full and frank disclosure of their financial circumstances. Failure to do this may not only result in a very annoyed judge, but could result in

79 Section 75(2) *Family Law Act 1975*.

that judge making adverse findings regarding the failure to disclose, and also very expensive costs orders against the party who failed to comply with the duty to make the disclosure. It also just drags the matter out needlessly and may make your ex's lawyer suspicious that you are hiding something, and so they may not only look a little closer than normal into what has been provided, but also start asking the court to issue subpoenas to your bank, the Australian Tax Office, your accountant, Sportsbet, the TAB, and possibly the casino closest to you for your membership to the high roller's club.

Lawyers can and do go through bank account statements and can and will find things like those funds you've transferred to a new partner or the hundreds and thousands spent on online gambling. In this way, usually we can trace the meals out with the new partner or the lingerie or adult toys bought on the joint credit card. Occasionally we find things like visits to brothels paid for on the credit card attached to the family business.

To be clear, we're not particularly interested in your sex life and there is nothing we have not seen before (and sometimes wish we could unsee), but if you're trying to convince a court that a post-separation credit card debt should be included, then payments to adult shops with your new partner are not going to help your case, or, indeed, your post-separation relationship with your ex.

Similarly, visits to brothels paid for on the company credit card will not help your argument that the business is all but insolvent. Finding a small fortune has been spent on gambling may also result in an pretty valid argument that your ex should get whatever is left, since you've had your fun already.

The net 'property pool'

In some matters, even establishing what the assets and liabilities are—the property pool—is a nightmare. Common problems are that you and your ex can't agree on ownership of assets, or the value of assets, or whether funds received from family were a loan or a gift. It can take quite a lot of patience to sift through bank accounts or layers of family trusts and companies to see where money has gone. This can be particularly difficult where there are family farms or companies and everyone weighs into the matter, and all of a sudden your second uncle twice removed is making a claim over the family farm.

If a party has sneakily transferred a property into their best friend's name, then you can expect the court will undo this transaction and probably make a costs order as well.

If a party has sold a property to a completely innocent third party who has nothing to do with any of this mess, then the court can take any losses incurred by the other party into account when making a property order.

As part of the duty of disclosure that we have discussed, each party must disclose what they actually own. A lawyer may also search registers such as land titles, share registers and the Australian Securities and Investments Commission (ASIC). A lawyer may comb through all available documents, so you can pretty much bet that if someone is hiding something, a family lawyer will find it. For example, it's always interesting when you find the signature of a spouse as a joint venture partner on a mortgage lodged with land titles, when the spouse is claiming that they have nothing to do with a major development that they were very involved in only twelve months before.

If you and your ex cannot agree on the value of property, then get it valued by a registered valuer early on. Valuers generally charge less than what you'll pay for a bunch of letters between lawyers arguing about the valuation of a house or your prized Holden Monaro. Market appraisals by real estate agents are not evidence of value, they are only indicative and useful in the early days of a separation as a guide to a property's value. Parties may agree to accept a market appraisal in mediation or in negotiations, but they are not good evidence for the court if the matter is being litigated. Only experts can give evidence of opinion and the opinion must be based on their particular expertise using the methodology appropriate to value the particular asset.[80]

Sometimes you and your ex won't even be able to agree on a valuer. If this happens, the panel approach works well. One party puts forward a panel of three registered valuers and the other

80 Makita (Australia) Pty Ltd v. Sprowles [2001] NSWCA 305 (14 September 2001).

party has seven days to nominate one of them; failing that, the first party nominates the valuer. Sometimes you need an order to force the other party to have property or chattels valued. This is frustrating because the court is most likely going to make that order and so it's all really just a waste of time and money.

Family lawyers like neat balance sheets showing the assets and liabilities with their values, preferably as valued by a registered valuer. That gives everyone something to work off and it's all admissible in court, if it comes to that.

As we've touched on already, sometimes a client will tell Rebekah that their ex owns four investment properties, a share portfolio and a Maserati but they themselves own nothing, because it's all in their ex's name. To which Rebekah answers that this doesn't matter one little tiny bit, unless, of course, all the assets were acquired before the marriage and there's an iron-clad pre-nup in place. Which usually they weren't and usually there isn't.

Any assets acquired during the relationship—and even before, in many cases—are considered part of the asset pool, regardless of which party's name it is in. Make sure that you tell your lawyer about every single one of your ex's assets, including cars, boats, share portfolios, property, artwork, businesses, tools of the trade, jewellery and household items (as well as your own).

Usually all assets are included in the property pool, no matter when or how they were obtained. There can be arguments about whether assets received by way of inheritance or after separation should be put in a separate property pool, but they will still be taken into account. So yes, your tools and your jewels are all part of the property pool, even if they were a gift from your ex to you.

If there is an argument about the value of such assets as jewels, cars, tools or furniture (also known as chattels), then get a joint valuation by a registered chattels valuer (now, there's a fun job in a growth industry!) This will save time and possibly money and give everyone a basis to negotiate from.

Usually, unless you have highly collectable cars or antiques, chattels are worth surprisingly little. Jewellery is generally worth less than a quarter of what you paid for it, which seems weird because there aren't really any one carat diamond rings for $2000 floating around (we know, because we've looked).

So, it is important to work out the property pool, which is done by using a list like this:

Asset/Liability	Ownership	Estimated value
Home: (address)		
Investment properties: (address/es)		
Motor vehicle/s: (year/make/model)		
Boat/s: (year/make/model)		
Cash in bank accounts: (account number/s)		
Investments: (type)		
Shares: (company/amount/type)		
Business: (name ABN)		
Chattels: (antiques, jewellery, tools, coins, furniture etc.—list)		
Rental bond: (Agent/landlord)		
Frequent flyer points:		

Asset/Liability	**Ownership**	**Estimated value**
Other points: (Myer, Woolworths etc.)		
Expected money from employment: (redundancies, long service leave that can be taken as cash, bonuses etc.)		
Liabilities:		
Home loan/s: (bank/account number/s)		
Investment property loan: (bank/account number/s)		
Investment loan: (bank/account number/s)		
Line of credit: (bank/account number/s)		
Credit cards: (bank/account number/s)		
Motor vehicle loans: (creditor/account number/s)		
Personal loans: (creditor/account number/s)		
Hire purchase/leases: (creditor/account numbers/s)		
Tax liabilities:		
School fees:		

Contributions

In considering what order to make (if any order is to be made), the court must consider contributions. These are:

- financial contributions made to the acquisition, conservation or improvement of any of the property, and these contributions can be from the sale of property, from income, a gift from a third party (such as a parent), an inheritance, compensation payment or redundancy
- non-financial contributions, such as renovations or working with no pay in a family business
- welfare contributions, including contributions made in the capacity of homemaker or parent.

Usually, in a long marriage where you may have been at home with the kids and your ex may have been working, or you both worked and parented at different times and in different ways, it will not matter to the court who did what. Unless someone brought in a lump sum from a pre-existing house or an inheritance, the court will generally consider your contributions to be 'equal or thereabouts'. The idea that one party could be said to have made a 'special contribution' because they were a very special and important super genius, whereas you were just a stay-at-home parent, has been emphatically rejected by the Family Court in most cases.[81]

Just to be clear—if you have been the stay-at-home parent, in the eyes of the court you have contributed just as much as the wage-earner. Rebekah has had matters where she has acted for a wife who was married for twenty or thirty years, who has been the stay-at-home parent of a gaggle of children, the bookkeeper of the family business and the general slave of the world for her family, only to have the husband suggest that as she didn't 'work', she shouldn't get anything. The court usually has other ideas.

Pre- and post-separation contributions can be important. For example, if you inherit a large amount of money before the relationship or late in the relationship or after separation, or you win the lottery, or you save a significant amount of money from your post-separation income, these funds may be treated as a separate pool.

---

81 *Kane & Kane* [2013] FamCAFC 205.

Future needs

The next thing that the court looks at is the factors set out in section 75(2) of the *Family Law Act 1975*, usually referred to as the future needs of each of the former couple. The importance of these factors will differ between cases involving short relationships with no children, and very long relationships with children.

In short relationships with no children, usually the relationship has not really changed either of the former couple's financial situations that much, so a disparity of income won't be that significant. Exceptions could be if the wife gave up a job so as to move to support the husband's job or to work in the family business.

In short relationships with children, the questions of who did the most caring for the child or children, and any disparity of income, will become important.

In lengthy relationships with children (whether the kids are now adults or not) there is traditionally a difference in income, if one of the couple has stayed at home and the other went out to work. Sometimes the primary earner is upset because they feel like they have sacrificed time with their kids in order to work, and now they are being 'punished'. Conversely, the primary parent/homemaker may be upset because they sacrificed their career and are now faced with an uncertain financial future. These are not easy questions to answer, but the court will take the view that consciously or unconsciously, the couple adopted certain roles in the relationship, which led to a difference in financial circumstances and must be addressed so that any orders are 'just and equitable'. It might be decided that the person in the weaker financial situation will get an 'adjustment' of between 5 to 20 per cent, so the final division of property is something like 60 per cent to the wife and 40 per cent to the husband.

Just and equitable

The final consideration is about stepping back and seeing if the orders are 'just and equitable' in all the circumstances. This can include whether there is any impact on earning capacity (if one of the assets being dealt with in the orders earns income, such as a family farm or business). Or, perhaps, it will become clear that one party is getting all of the tangible assets, like two houses and the car, and the other is just getting super, and that this may not be exactly fair.

Case study—John and Jane

John and Jane had been married for twenty years and had two boys together. John was a public servant and Jane a personal assistant. Jane stopped working for a while when the boys were born and then returned to work part time so that she could still get the boys to their football training and music lessons.

John and Jane were both active in the community and supported groups like the boys' school and local football club. Jane was on the school parents' committee and John was on the committee for the football club.

When they separated, the boys were adults and John and Jane had a total non-superannuation pool of $720 000 (they owned their home outright and it was worth $500 000, had some savings, of $200 000, and cars worth about $10 000). John had a lot more super than Jane. John was also earning $200 000 and Jane $50 000. After a hearing, the judge decided that it was just and equitable for the super to be equalised and, regarding the rest of the property, for Jane to receive 60 per cent of the property pool and John to receive 40 per cent. The outcome looked like this (John needed to borrow money to pay Jane, as John wanted to keep the house):

Non-super:

To John		**To Jane**	
Home	$500 000	Existing cash	$200 000
Car	$10 000	Car	$10 000
John must pay Jane	-$222 000	Jane receives from John	$222 000
Total	$288 000	Total	$432 000
	40 per cent		60 per cent

Super:

John		**Jane**	
John's super	$450 000	John's super	$50 000
Amount to Jane	-$200 000	From John	$200 000
New total	$250 000	New total	$250 000

Common questions and issues in property matters

We know this is all a bit complicated. Like much of family law, how property matters are determined really depends on the circumstances of your case. But in every property matter, we see the same issues coming up all the time. Here we've summarised the more frequently asked questions.

Can I get a stamp duty exemption?

Each of the Australian states and territories has an exemption from paying stamp duty on the sale of a property if the transfer of property from joint names to one name, or from one name to another name, is done because of a BFA or court order (including consent orders). For example, if you buy your ex out of your joint property, their name will be removed from the title, and ordinarily stamp duty would be payable on that transaction unless you are eligible for the exemption.

Case study—Fred and Jamie

Fred and Jamie had been in a de facto relationship for ten years. When their relationship ended, Fred made Jamie an offer that he would buy Jamie out of the home they shared. The house was in their joint names, and so after finalising their BFA, the transfer of the home into Fred's sole name was exempt, and Fred saved a substantial amount of money.

Stamp duty can, of course, be more expensive than the cost of getting a BFA or a consent order, so this is a really important consideration, especially when stamp duty on some houses can be $100 000 or more.

Because stamp duty is a state and territory tax, the schemes differ slightly, and it's important that you make sure the arrangements you enter into will attract a stamp duty exemption. Your lawyer can help you with this, or you can find out more by googling 'stamp duty exemption family law' and then the name of your state or territory.

Is it a gift? Is it a loan? No, it's a mess!

It is very common, especially in these times of high property prices, for parents to give money to an adult child to help them buy a house. Everyone merrily assumes that they all knew what each other meant. Usually when there is then a separation, one party suddenly discovers that the money was 'always' going to be repaid to the parents if the home was sold.

These cases cause endless litigation and high levels of emotion and therefore are super expensive. They can also cause huge problems within extended families as everyone gets to stick their two cents in. This does not bode well for those times when you need everyone to turn up and pretend to play happy families, such as at weddings and graduations.

Unless everyone has an attack of the reasonables, it is up to the judge hearing the case to decide whether the funds were a loan or a gift (and therefore a contribution made on behalf of the party receiving it) and whether the funds should be repaid on the sale of an asset. Judges have discretion, but they are also guided by past cases. The Family Court has found that it is up to the judge to decide whether the allegation that a loan is a loan and not a gift is true,[82] and the judge will look at things like:

- Is there a loan agreement clearly setting out everyone's rights and responsibilities?
- Is the loan registered as a mortgage?
- Has there been any acceptance in writing by either party that it was a loan?
- Have regular repayments been made?

82 Biltoft [1995] FamCA 45.

- Have homes been sold after the funds were received, with no demand for repayment?
- Were similar amounts given to other siblings?
- Were wills amended to reflect the gift?

Usually it is not clear cut—some things will suggest loan, some things will suggest gift.

The only thing that is certain is that it will be very, very expensive to try to sort it out as it will take many affidavits, days in court and arguments for the judge to get to the bottom of it all. One thing is for sure, no one will be happy. The same issues arise if a parent dies and the other siblings suddenly realise that one sibling received a heap of money.

Case study—Tina and Michael

Tina and Michael were married for ten years. Four years into the marriage, Tina's mother, Meredith, gave Tina $500 000, as an 'early inheritance'. Meredith had sold the family home and downsized, and so wanted to help Tina and Michael establish themselves. Tina and Michael used the money to buy a home in Sydney's inner west, which they otherwise would not have been able to afford.

When the marriage ended a year later, Michael proposed a fifty-fifty property split. Tina resisted this, arguing (eventually in court) that the $500 000 given to her by her mother was hers alone.

The fact that it was a gift solely to Tina and was specified as an inheritance given early, in text messages between Tina and Meredith, became crucial to the case. The court found that the money was only meant to be given to Tina, not Michael, and so was excluded from the property pool.

'Stolen' assets

If you think your ex is hiding assets, has a secret bank account, has regularly been taking trips to the Cayman Islands, is an international drug lord, or seems to be spending a lot of time in his mistress's suspiciously new $2 million apartment, then a forensic accountant can help you find the money and get your fair share of it. A forensic accountant is a specialist accountant who provides advice that is admissible (that is, can be used as evidence) in court.

Your lawyer will have a forensic accountant they use—if you're in this situation, and you think there's a fair bit of cash you don't know about, then you must get a lawyer. Don't self-represent in these circumstances, because if there's money being hidden, you can bet your ex will have a lawyer.

If the judge comes to the conclusion that it is more probable than not that a party has hidden assets away, then they can divide what is left accordingly—even to the extent of giving the innocent party everything else.

My ex has spent all the money on gambling/drinking/who knows what

You can't get blood out of a stone, and if your ex has indeed spent all the money, and there are no other assets, then there's not a huge amount you can do except take up voodoo and hope the karma bus gets them. If there are some assets left, then the court can, in certain circumstances, make orders that you get all or most of whatever is left.

If assets have been given away, the court can undo that or make orders that you get more or all of whatever is left. The same can apply if assets have been wasted on purpose or recklessly wasted (such as on extravagant, first class overseas holidays), as long as there are money or assets left to be divided.

My ex won't pay our kids' school fees—what do I do?

The court takes the view that children are entitled to a public school education, and if parents cannot afford private school fees, then the kids cannot go to a private school. This can be a really hard situation, especially if the kids have to be pulled out of the school.

If there was a clear agreement that the children go to a particular school, and the parents can demonstrably afford the fees, then the DHS can change the child support assessment to make it so.[83] This will probably require a special assessment, which we talked about in Chapter 7.

It's also worth talking to the school—if your child is in year eleven and only has a little while to go, the school will often agree to let you pay the money back over a period of time, or might agree to a bursary—so long as your kid hasn't been a right little pest for the past five and a half years, that is!

My ex cut off my access to our joint bank account—what can I do?

Firstly, don't panic; they have probably been told to do this by their lawyer or they read about it on some website. You must go and see your bank as soon as possible if your ex has done something sneaky like change all the passwords for your accounts. If your name is on that account, you can have your access reinstated. You can also request that the account is made subject to a 'two to sign' requirement so your ex can't take all the money and move to Ipanema.

You can also see a lawyer or community legal service and make a formal request for spousal maintenance (which we've talked about earlier) if you are unable to live in the meantime, particularly if you're a stay-at-home parent and your ex has stopped paying their wages into your joint account.

83 www.humanservices.gov.au/customer/forms/cs1970.

My ex has run up a huge credit card bill post our split and says I have to pay it—what are my rights?

Let's be clear here, the court has to make orders that are 'just and equitable'. Paying for your ex's new Jimmy Possum furniture, legal fees, his RSVP account or her meals out with her new boyfriend will not be okay (and believe us, these will show up on the statements—hilariously sometimes the RSVP charges come *after* the meals out with the new partner, leading to some very awkward scenes in mediation when the ex has brought the new partner along for 'support' and we all go through the credit card statements together).

Unless there is a court order saying differently, each party bears their own costs, and unless there was an agreement, paying for legal fees from joint funds will usually result in that money being returned to your ex, if there is any money left.

No court is going to make you pay for your ex's spending spree. They will be responsible for their own post-separation credit card debt unless it is reasonable expenditure for the benefit of the family. Any such expenditure from joint accounts will come out of their cut of the money (if—and it's a big if—there is any left).

We have no assets and a lot of debt—what happens now?

This can be very difficult as there must be property for the court to have the power to make orders about how that property is divided. You can't divide nothing. (There's some maths equation about that, isn't there?)

Usually parties have some superannuation at the very least and this gives the court the ability to alter property interests, but sometimes there's no money or assets at all. The court cannot magic up assets to satisfy a debt or to provide a settlement.

This is because the power of the court to make orders comes from the legislation, and the legislation talks about making orders about altering property interests. The court can make orders that a party refinance a debt, or that an asset be sold to pay down debt, or that a party be solely responsible for a debt.

If your ex has no money or assets, then you may simply be throwing good money after bad by spending more on legal bills. It is a cost-benefit analysis of whether it is worth pursuing them, and if there's no money, then it's probably not worth it.

'I'd rather pay the lawyer than my ex' and other lunatic ideas

A very easy trap to fall into is spending a great deal of money on trying to 'beat' your former spouse in court. One or both parties may decide that they're going to spend every cent they have, and quite a bit more on top, in order to 'win' against their ex. The thing is, nobody gets a trophy at the end of litigation. You just get a bill from your lawyer. We've all heard stories about people who litigate for years over a tea set. These sorts of people don't need lawyers, they (genuinely) need a psychologist.

Case study—Annabel and Tom

Annabel had been married to Tom for twenty-five years before she finally left, and eventually filed for divorce. It was a bitterly unhappy marriage at the end, marred by infidelity and horrible fighting. The couple had four children, two of whom still lived at home, and assets in excess of $4 million.

The marital home was a five-bedroom estate in the Perth suburb of Subiaco, and both Annabel and Tom were highly paid medical professionals, but a protracted legal battle resulted in each party walking away with less than $500 000 each—just enough for them to both buy a townhouse in neighbouring suburbs. Tom had lawyered up first, furious with Annabel for leaving him, and Annabel returned fire, angry with Tom over an affair he had at the end of the marriage, and the matter eventually went to the High Court for determination on an obscure point of law.

Their combined legal bills were over $2 million and the matter raged on for more than ten years. Had Annabel and Tom agreed to a fair division of the assets early in their separation without engaging in litigated warfare with each other, they would have each gotten at least $1 million more.

We have a huge mortgage and my ex is refusing to pay it

If your ex has moved out of the family home, and the mortgage is in joint names, it often comes as astonishing news that they can simply stop paying their share (or the whole thing, if you have been a stay-at-home parent and your ex's wages paid the mortgage).

If you default on the mortgage (in other words, you stop paying it), your lending institution can (and will) call in the loan. That is, they can force the sale of the house, and you'll be left with whatever is left over after the bank has taken their money and any other fees you have incurred. You'll also get a black mark on your credit rating. Banks generally engage very expensive lawyers (even more expensive than your lawyer) and you get to cover this cost as well.

This is the worst-case scenario. To avoid this, if you're in the position where your ex has moved out and won't help pay the mortgage, talk to your bank or credit union. They don't want you to default. They want to help you sort out your situation so they get their money without a lot of tedious extra paperwork. Your lender will have a process to help you get your finances in order until you work out a temporary agreement with your ex, or a final agreement where you either buy your ex out of the house or your ex buys you out of the house, or you sell the house and divide the proceeds with your ex according to your settlement.

Generally the court would expect someone to pay for outgoings (including the mortgage) on a home that they are living in. This expectation can change if you simply cannot afford to pay those outgoings on your own and there is a large disparity of earnings between you and your ex.

Sometimes separations occur where one party is a stay-at-home parent and there are good reasons why they should stay in the home with the children but they cannot afford the mortgage (for example, the house has been modified to be compliant with disability standards for your special needs child). If this is the case for you, and your ex is simply refusing to pay the mortgage, seek advice regarding whether you should apply for urgent spousal maintenance. Spousal maintenance is ordered when one party can afford to pay it and the other party has a need for it because they cannot support themselves due to having to take care of children, or because of advanced age or health reasons. The court must not take into account a means-tested Australian pension when working out if a party has a need for or an ability to pay spousal maintenance.

Child support, which is separate from spousal support, can take a long time to start to be received and this can be extremely scary for the receiving parent. Apply for child support early and get advice if you are being asked to agree to child support being paid as mortgage payments or school fees.

Another option is to sell the home immediately if you can't possibly pay the mortgage by yourself. In this situation, the proceeds of the sale will be held in trust (by your lawyers) until after final settlement of your property matter, when it is then distributed according to your agreement.

It's also worth noting that any repayments your ex makes on the mortgage if you have sole occupation of the house may be seen as post-separation contributions and may be taken into account when the settlement is calculated.

Who keeps the pets?

In family law, companion animals are classified as property. Therefore, who gets to keep Fluffy and Rex is a matter of dividing property, and the court can make an order as to who gets to keep the cat or dog or snake or fish. The court considers a few things in assessing who should keep the pets, and these include:

- who has looked after the animal the most (walked it, took it to the vet, fed it and cleaned up after it)
- whose name the animal is registered in
- who can best look after the animal in the new family arrangements (i.e. if you live in an apartment and you're

fighting over a horse with your ex, who lives on a farm, you might not win that one)

- any other factors, such as if the dog is a working dog or the cat is the offspring of the childhood pet of one of the parties.

The court will then make an assessment on the facts, will award the animal some nominal sum as a value (unless it's a very expensive working dog or show cat), and an order will be made that the animal is the property of one of the parties.

Often, the decision as to who keeps the pets is extremely fraught and not as easy as it appears from the factors above. We've heard of a couple who stay together by having an agreement that whoever leaves the marriage first gets the kids, and the other person gets the dog.

Many of us see our animals as family, including us—we have three dogs, four cats and a macaw between us—and the idea of losing your animals is heartbreaking. Lots of separated families get around this by 'sharing custody' of the pets—easier when the pet is a dog—so that the dog goes with the kids between houses. This is less easy when your pet is a horse.

It's also important to be aware that many people stay in abusive relationships because they are afraid that their animals will be hurt if they leave. Many organisations are trying to help those in this situation, and some women's refuges will take pets. 1800RESPECT can help you make a safety plan to leave an abusive relationship in such a way that your pets will also be protected.

Leaving the marital home

One of the toughest times of divorcing (we seem to say that a lot in this book) is selling or leaving your family home. Sadly, it's the reality for many separating people. There's very often just not enough money to be able to rehouse both parties without downsizing or moving to a different, cheaper area. But that doesn't mean it doesn't massively hurt. You have probably worked really hard for your home, and you probably love it. You don't have to own it to love it—it can be just as hard to leave your rented home.

Many people won't realise the depth of your pain at having to leave your home. They just think, 'Well, that's what divorce is!' but housing insecurity is the major reason many people stay in terrible relationships far longer than they should. The insane cost of housing in many Australian cities and towns is a huge impediment to being able to leave even the worst of marriages.

Legally, whether or not you sell your house after separation comes down to a few things. Can your former partner buy you out of your home? Can you buy your former partner out of your home? How do you feel about taking on a potentially huge mortgage, that you expected to be paying as part of a couple, by yourself?

When your property settlement is being worked through, it will become clearer whether or not you'll be able to stay in your home. It's not the case that assets are automatically split fifty-fifty—there's a very complicated formula for working the division out, which your lawyer will help you with. It all depends on contributions, both financial and non-financial, and things like being the primary carer of small children are taken very much into account, as is superannuation!

No matter what happens in terms of the property, you'll be very worried about the kids being disrupted, and if you're the one leaving, it can be an enormous source of guilt when you know you're the reason (no matter how good your reasons are) why the kids have to leave their home and possibly their schools, friends and community.

Staying in the marital home

This can also be a difficult thing, but, of course, being able to stay in your community at a time of horrible upheaval can be a great relief. At the same time, you're surrounded by memories of your defunct relationship, good and bad—remember when you bought that couch together? Remember when you threw the mug at that wall and left that dent? Remember having that huge fight over the new TV unit at the Homemaker Centre? Good times, good times.

Additionally, you may have a new mortgage so high you can barely jump over it, and the thought of being solely responsible for all those zeros will keep you awake at night.

A point to consider here—it might be worth thinking about selling if you're finding your mortgage stress is crippling (mortgage stress is where more than 30 per cent of your weekly earnings after tax are going to your housing costs). You don't have to give yourself a nervous breakdown trying to stay in your home if it's too hard. It might be better for you, and your children, to live in a smaller home with a more manageable mortgage than to make yourself sick with anxiety and overwork.

If the home is going to have to be sold, then do it as part of your settlement, because then the costs of sale will be shared. If you end up having to sell six months later, then you may end up paying the real estate agent's $25 000 commission yourself, and that's not fair.

As we mentioned earlier in this chapter, if you transfer a property from joint names to your sole name, or from your ex's name to your name because there are court orders or a financial agreement, then the transfer should be exempt from stamp duty. Sometimes it is well worth transferring property to save the costs of sale (real estate agents and conveyancing fees) and to save having to pay stamp duty on a new home.

When you have the good luck and terrible misfortune of staying in your home, one thing that can help is mixing it up as much as you can. We know that money might be tighter than ever, but even moving furniture around can help, or adding new pillows and throws from Kmart or Target. Getting new bed linen is a priority—no need to sleep in the same sheets, after all!

Tips and traps

When you're negotiating your property settlement, it can be very hard to remain cool, calm and collected, while still fighting for your fair share. We've seen clients forget to mention key assets (this rarely ends well), or give up things they're entitled to, just to make the matter go away.

While it's important to give and take in order to reach an outcome, don't forget to divide, or at least take account of, the following easily overlooked items:

- superannuation—yes, this is property and, yes, the orders can equalise or otherwise 'split' (divide) super
- frequent flier points—these are actually quite lucrative and even if you've been a stay-at-home parent/spouse while your partner has been a corporate high-flyer, you'll probably be entitled to at least half of these points
- credit card points—if you or your ex paid all the household expenses on a credit card, then there may be thousands of dollars in points on that card
- hotel memberships that accumulate points (also lucrative)
- any long-term incentives and short-term incentives that form part of your ex's salary package (also known as bonuses)
- any share allocations you or your ex receives as part of your salary package
- iTunes or Spotify accounts—these can be worth thousands and thousands of dollars—and these days, can be worth as much as traditional music collections, if not more
- long service leave—if this is available as a cash payment, then it is property that can be divided; if it is available only as leave, then it is important to take it into account, as it is guaranteed income
- Defence Force Retirement and Death Benefits Scheme (DFRDB)—you should seek legal advice if you or your ex has a DFRDB pension
- if it applies, try to reach an agreement on airport lounge access memberships, especially if you'll be travelling frequently with your children. While it won't be relevant to everyone, in many divorces one or both spouses are corporate types, with significant perks of the job that their ex won't want to lose. Most of these memberships also

extend to the spouse. You should ask your lawyer to negotiate you staying on your former spouse's membership for as long as possible (one couple we know did this until the wife remarried).

Enforcing property orders

So you have negotiated hard and fair and you have sealed orders or a fully executed financial agreement. Or you have been through the trauma of a trial and the judge has made orders. What happens if your ex simply does not comply with them?

If you are to be paid a lump sum of money or periodic payments of money, then interest is payable if you are not paid. The interest rate is the Reserve Bank of Australia target cash rate that is published on 1 January and 1 July each year plus 6 per cent.[84]

If you are to be paid a lump sum and a property is to be transferred into your ex's sole name, then hopefully there are default sale provisions. This means if your ex is unable or unwilling to pay you, or to refinance the mortgage into their sole name, the home is sold so you can be paid and the mortgage can be discharged.

Hopefully there is also an order that the registrar can sign a document if a party refuses to, and some default sale orders. If your ex will not (or cannot) pay you, then you can trigger the default sale orders. If they refuse to cooperate, then the registrar of the court can sign documents like contracts for sale or a discharge of mortgage and/or you can ask the court to appoint a trustee for sale.

If a home is being transferred into one party's sole name and the other party is being paid out, it is good practice to have default sale orders, especially if the party receiving the property has to refinance a mortgage. Post-GFC and with the tightening of lending practices, sometimes, through nobody's fault, the person taking the property and the mortgage can't get finance. If there are no default sale orders, then it is back to the negotiating table or back to court to try to get the orders enforced.

84 www.familycourt.gov.au/wps/wcm/connect/fcoaweb/rules-and-legislation/rate-of-interest/.

While the court has the power to enforce orders, including changing the parts of the orders that make the orders work,[85] appointing trustees for sale, and even imprisonment (yes, really—judges don't like people ignoring their orders),[86] this can be expensive and time consuming. Default sale orders can protect both parties.

Case study—Bob and Amy

Bob and Amy worked out a property settlement and were pretty amicable. Bob was going to keep the family home, refinance the mortgage and pay Amy out. Since they were amicable, they didn't think they needed to have backup orders about what would happen if Bob wasn't able to refinance the mortgage or make the payment to Amy. Tragically, about a week after the consent orders were made, Bob was hit by a bus as he was cycling to work. He was in hospital for a very long time and was not able to refinance the mortgage or pay Amy out. In fact, he was not able to make any decisions about his financial affairs for a few months and there was no enduring power of attorney in place. In the end, Amy reluctantly took the matter to court and new orders were made.

The lesson here is that things do go wrong, people do get hit by buses, and you have to have workable alternatives in place.

85 Kaljo & Kaljo [1978] FLC 90-445.
86 PDM & JEM [2006] FamCA 1182 (8 November 2006).

WORKSHEET 6
QUESTIONS FOR MY LAWYER REGARDING MY PROPERTY SETTLEMENT

Once again, this worksheet is so you can jot down any questions you have for your lawyer before you go into the meeting or teleconference. Remembering that lawyers charge up to $600 an hour in six-minute units, it's very important that you don't waste your money by not having a really clear idea of what questions you want answered.

Date:	**Date:**
Questions for my lawyer regarding my property settlement	**Answers**
1.	
2.	
3.	
4.	
5.	
6.	
7.	
8.	
9.	

10

The first year and filing for divorce

NOTE—once you have a final divorce order from the court, you only have a year to make an application to the court for property and/or spousal maintenance orders. You can ask the court for an extension but this is not always given, and it can end up costing you more money.

A year has passed, and you've survived to tell the tale. (Which you probably do, over and over again, to anyone who will listen. And that's totally fine and a completely natural response—it's how healthy people process trauma.)

At the one-year mark you've probably started to settle into your 'new normal' and you've got a bit of a routine going with your ex in terms of co-parenting, if you have kids. Hopefully you've got the property settlement well underway, and child support is being paid regularly with no fighting.

So now is the time that you can start to think about filing for divorce. In Australia, you must be separated for twelve months and one day before you can file for a **divorce order**. A divorce order is made but only becomes final a month after—just in case you both change your mind and decide to get back together. Once the order becomes final, you are both free to remarry.

Divorce order—an order made by a court that ends a marriage.

Obviously, do not remarry before the divorce order is made final, as not only will the new marriage be invalid, you may also get arrested for bigamy and you'll probably make the news (which might have the bonus of making your seven-year-old's YouTube channel a bit more interesting).

The twelve-month-and-one-day (don't forget the one day—the court will reject the application if it is filed a day too early) separation period need not be twelve continuous months. If you reconcile briefly (for three or fewer months) the twelve-month period does not have to start all over again, but can be calculated using the time before the reconciliation and the time after the reconciliation (not the time you were both reconciled). For example, Simon and Ophelia separated in August. In late October they got back together for two months, splitting again just after Christmas. Their date of separation remains as August, but the twelve months is now up in the October of the following year.

If you were separated under the same roof, this may be able to be counted towards the separation period but you will both need to agree that you were actually separated. Being separated means not sharing a bed, not being intimate with each other, not socialising as a couple and not living together as a couple. Doing basic housework and preparing meals for each other is okay, especially if you have kids. If you are making a sole application, you will need to include some independent proof, like an affidavit from a friend or relative.

If you have been married for less than two years, you will have to go to counselling to consider reconciliation before you make an application for a divorce order, unless there are special circumstances (such as violence or abuse). A counsellor must provide a certificate and this certificate can say that the parties have tried counselling, or that counselling was not appropriate. A Family Relationship Centre can provide the counselling and they can be found at the following website: http://www.familyrelationships.gov.au/Services/Pages/default.aspx.

If one or both of you have a new partner, you're probably keen to get the process underway. Your ex may even have asked you to falsify the date of your separation on your filing papers to get the divorce underway sooner (probably so they can remarry, gross). Don't do this. It's a legal document and it's swearing a false statement, which is an offence.

If you don't have new partners, then oftentimes filing for divorce might be put off for a while. There's no legal requirement that separated people actually get a divorce and there's no legal rush, it's not like doing your taxes! There's also no requirement that you have to consent to the divorce. In this chapter, we'll look at all the ins and outs, complicated legal issues, and other tips and traps relating to divorce.

How do I file for divorce?

Filing for divorce is actually pretty easy, and you can do it yourself if you want to. Go to www.federalcircuitcourt.gov.au/wps/wcm/connect/fccweb/how-do-i/apply-for-a-divorce/apply-for-divorce.

You can file for a divorce jointly with your ex or on your own. If you make an application for a divorce on your own and you have children under eighteen, you will need to go to the court, as the court must be satisfied that proper arrangements have been made for the children. The court can ask for a family report to be done if they're concerned that proper provisions for the children haven't been made.

What is a joint application and a sole application?

A joint application means that you both agree to the divorce, and you both sign the application form. The application doesn't have to be served on either party and if you have children under eighteen you usually won't have to go to court.

A sole application is made by one spouse only. You will need to serve the application on your ex and if you have children under eighteen you will need to go to court to satisfy the registrar that your ex has been served, that the court has jurisdiction, that you have been separated for over twelve months and that proper arrangements have been made for your children.

Do I have to consent to the divorce?

You do not need to consent, but it is likely that if the application has been filled out properly, and if there are no major issues such as an international court being the better place to hear the matter, then the divorce order will be made.

Some people (who fall under the 'mad' category in the 'mad, bad and sad' risk assessment) turn up and inform the court that they do not have jurisdiction to grant a divorce because it was a marriage under God and they are not God and so cannot tear it asunder. This will not prevent the registrar making the order, no matter how earnestly this belief is held. These are the same people who think that writing 'a natural person' on all their letters somehow makes a legal difference to their matter. It doesn't.

Who pays, and how much does it cost?

The filing fees are pretty steep (as at October 2017 $865), and you may be entitled for a reduction of fees, bringing the filing fee down to $290, if you receive a Centrelink benefit, for example. If it is a joint application, then you both must be entitled to the reduction of fees in order to receive it.

If you are making the application on your own, then you will have to pay the whole fee. If it is a joint application, then usually you share it with your ex.

Service of the application

If you are making a sole application for divorce, then you will need to have it personally served on your ex, if you think that your ex will not sign an acknowledgement of service. It is best to have a professional process server carry out the work. Your lawyer can find a process server for you. You could have a friend do the job, but this may put your friend in an awkward situation.

Sometimes people disappear and cannot be found even by a process server. In these circumstances your lawyer can help you.

Rebekah has recently had a matter where she was representing the husband, and where the court was satisfied that the wife knew about the proceedings because she sent a nasty message back to Rebekah on her professional Facebook page.

Checklist for the newly separated/divorced person

You'll have a lot of things that you'll need to remember to change, such as bank account names, your mortgage, and addresses if you've moved. But there are a few things you might not think of, which might not be readily obvious. Make sure:

- Your private health insurance policy has been transferred to your name (and your kids are included on it).
- Your car insurance details are transferred to your name. Lucy didn't realise there was a difference between compulsory third party and comprehensive insurance—not until she backed into a brand-new Range Rover and discovered she hadn't transferred her comprehensive cover over, anyway.
- Your car registration has been transferred into your name and new address. Some exes can be very unpleasant and not pass on penalty notices, meaning you end up with even bigger fines, or worse, pulled over by the local constabulary because your licence has been suspended.
- You've informed Centrelink of your separation and updated your income estimate (this should have been done within two weeks of you separating, but it's worth the reminder).
- You have transferred your Medicare details onto your own new card, along with your children's.
- You have notified the children's school or daycare of your separation and asked for report cards to be sent to both parents, and for all notices to be sent to both parents.
- The Foxtel or Netflix account has been put in your name. There's nothing worse than ringing up because the bloody

Netflix won't load when you're halfway through *Offspring* and they won't talk to you because 'I'm sorry, but you're not the account holder'.

- You have updated your toll-road accounts. One woman we know inadvertently paid her ex-husband's tolls for three years.

Moving on

At some point, the odds are very high that you will find new love. The birds will sing, and all of a sudden love songs on the radio will start making sense again. However, be aware that finding new love can be one of the most difficult things in terms of your ongoing relationship with your ex, particularly if there are kids involved. Studies show that even when things were quite amicable, the arrival of a new partner on the scene can make things very icy with your ex all over again.[87]

The best advice we ever got from our dad the divorce lawyer is to treat your ex like your business partner—someone with whom you are managing the very important business of raising your children together. Now, say you're quite keen to go into a new joint venture with someone else in a new business. Your business partner in your first business is going to be a bit worried about this. What will it mean for your old business? What does it mean for your shareholders (your children)? How will you manage the conflicts of interest?

Possibly pushing the analogy too far, you have to see your ex as a crucial stakeholder in your various businesses (the old and the new) and assure them that you've got a plan for how you're going to handle it. In business, communication is key. Don't let your first business partner read about your new associate on Facebook. Don't rub their nose in your exciting new joint venture.

It's just good business sense to be a bit respectful and discreet, at least until the dust settles. Research shows that most disputes over new partners occur within the first twelve months of the original couple separating, but substantially decrease after that time. The

87 www.aifs.gov.au/publications/family-matters/issue-92/effects-co-parenting-relationships-ex-spouses-couples-step.

first flush of new love can make us all do crazy things, so make sure you remember at all times to be the Sane Parent, even when your hormones are telling you that you *must* spend all your time with your new soul mate.

It's all very well and good to have an amicable divorce but it's quite another thing to have another man take your son to cricket training or have another woman brushing your daughter's hair. It hurts. Be respectful, and take it slow. Keep your exciting new business on the down low for a little while—and enjoy it!

WORKSHEET 7
QUESTIONS FOR MY LAWYER ABOUT FILING FOR DIVORCE

As we've discussed before, it's really important before each meeting or telephone conference with your lawyer that you have a clear idea of what questions you want to ask, in order to get the best value for your money. This worksheet is a space where you can write down your questions, and make notes of the answers you get.

Date:	**Date:**
Questions for my lawyer about filing for divorce	**Answers**
1.	
2.	
3.	
4.	
5.	
6.	
7.	
8.	
9.	
10.	

11

Thriving in your new life

It's over, just about. And haven't you just had the best time? No, you haven't, you poor thing. But you have made it. And you've probably got a pretty amazing playlist of 'I Will Survive'-type songs to go with it.

So, well done you. Probably by now your life is looking very different from how it looked when you were married. You might have (in no particular order):

- changed your kids' schools
- changed jobs or negotiated more family-friendly hours
- finalised your property settlement
- finalised your parenting plans
- sold the family home
- rented a new home
- bought a new home
- bought a new car
- taken up new hobbies

- returned to university or other formal education
- been in the midst of a family law court battle (poor you)
- finalised your divorce
- repartnered
- had to create a new co-parenting relationship with your ex
- dealt civilly with your ex on a regular basis.

It's a lot, isn't it?

Probably you'll look back on this time of your life as one of the hardest things you've ever had to go through. And it's not something that you get over easily, or quickly. But you've probably really grown as a person, too.

A good friend of ours learnt to drive later in life than most of her friends—she got her licence when she was twenty-two. She was a very anxious driver and tried to do it as little driving as possible. But when she was suddenly single, she had no choice but to drive, and to drive a lot. Her mother lived an hour and a half away, along Sydney's M5 (the scariest road in Australia, in our opinion) and if she wanted to see her (which she did), she'd have to drive there. Four years later she's an extremely confident driver (possibly overly confident) and manages peak-hour city traffic daily. It's such a small thing but a big deal for her—she never thought of herself as a competent driver and now she knows she is.

You might find yourself to be a totally different person from the person you were when you were married. You might have found new love, and you might be living in a new house with new stepchildren. You might find that while your life was turned upside down, you've made it even better than before.

You might have gotten a dog (your ex hated dogs), you might have gotten a cat (your ex was allergic to cats). You might have had to move houses, but perhaps you're finding that life is better than ever in your own little home where you don't have to walk on egg-shells all the time.

Rebekah rediscovered the joy of running—it kept her sane during year twelve and it did the same again after her separation. Not only has she now done three marathons and a whole lot of half marathons, she found a fantastic community and an incredibly supportive bunch of girlfriends at her local parkrun and has thrived as a result.[88]

You might still be grieving the life you imagined, or the life you planned. For some, divorce means the end of the dream to create a family, or to have more children. It might mean financial insecurity at an age when you thought you would be comfortably well off. It might mean having to share grandparenting duties with your ex-spouse at a time when you had dreamed of enjoying them together. Having said that, re-prosecuting every aspect of your failed marriage, and holding on to your anger and grief, can be very destructive.

If you find that you're still very upset and angry with your former spouse after a few years have passed, or if you're finding that you're still fighting with your former spouse over things like respecting each other's boundaries, it can be very helpful to speak with a counsellor, who can give you strategies to reduce your emotional responses to your ex.

Boundaries and mutual respect are the best tools at your disposal to help you form a productive and, yes, amicable relationship with your ex, particularly if you have children. The ultimate goal is to get to the acceptance stage of grief—indeed, to no longer be grieving, because you've well and truly moved on.

The most useful advice we ever heard was from a psychologist who said, 'We're all just fancy monkeys trying to do our best', which sums up the futility of trying to work out why people do the things they do. It took time, and patience, and good will on all sides, but both Rebekah and Lucy have functional co-parenting relationships with their former husbands. It can be done.

Divorce isn't easy. It has decades-long ramifications. But with a bit of bravery, you can remake your life to be yours, and it can be a great life. Remember, you're divorced *from* your ex, you're not divorced *to* them.

88 www.parkrun.com.au.

As JK Rowling, the patron saint of divorced people, said, 'Rock bottom became the solid foundation on which I rebuilt my life'. And so it can be for you.

We know, because it was for us.

WORKSHEET 8
WHAT HAVE YOU FOUND OUT ABOUT YOURSELF AFTER YOUR SEPARATION?

Things I was afraid of	Things I now can do	Things I've learnt	Things I want to do

Glossary

Abuse—in relation to a child, means:

- an assault, including a sexual assault, of the child
- a person (the first person) involving the child in a sexual activity with the first person or another person in which the child is used, directly or indirectly, as a sexual object by the first person or the other person, and where there is unequal power in the relationship between the child and the first person
- causing the child to suffer serious psychological harm, including (but not limited to) when that harm is caused by the child being subjected to, or exposed to, family violence or
- serious neglect of the child.

Address for service—the physical street address, or email address, given by a party (generally you, or your ex) where legal documents can be served on you or your ex by hand, post or some other form of electronic communication.

Adjourn—change or postpone a court event (i.e. any time you or your lawyer has to go to court for your case) to another day or time.

Affidavit—a written legal statement by a party or witness. An affidavit is a legal version of 'he said, she said'. It's how you present the facts of your case to the court. You must have an affidavit signed before an authorised person (such as a lawyer or Justice of the Peace), and you must swear to or attest to the truth of the contents of the affidavit when you speak in court about what you've said in your affidavit. It is an offence to lie in an affidavit. Learning to spell affidavit (and subpoena) takes up almost an entire semester of law school. It's pronounced 'affa-day-vit'.

Appeal—a procedure that allows a party to challenge the decision made by a court to a higher court. It takes a long time and costs a lot of money to appeal a decision.

Applicant—the person who applies to a court for orders (which means a decision is made and then turned into legally enforceable orders).

Case—when a person makes an application to a court for orders, that becomes the case before the court. It can also be called your 'matter', but generally only before it becomes a 'case'. We like to keep you on your toes.

Case law—law that has been made by a judge or judges, which is binding, and becomes precedent (see Precedent). (Also see unhelpful.)

Conference—a meeting between lawyers and their clients, or between lawyers and the judge.

Consent order—an agreement between the parties (generally about the children or finances in family law) that is approved by the court and then becomes a legally enforceable court order.

Contravention—when a court finds a party has not followed a court order (including consent orders), that party is in contravention of (broken the terms of) the order. There are penalties that apply to contraventions of a court order, which can range from a fine to possibly imprisonment.

Court hearing—the date and time when a case is scheduled to come before the court.

Court order—the actions the parties or a party must do to carry out a decision made by a court. An order may be either interim or final. Interim means that it's not yet finalised, but must be followed until it is finalised.

Divorce order—an order made by a court that ends a marriage.

Enforcement order—an order made by a court to make a party or person comply with (that is, follow) an order.

Ex parte hearing—a hearing where one party is not present and has not been given notice of the application before the court; usually reserved for urgent cases (like where there's a risk of international child abduction).

Family consultant—a psychologist and/or social worker who specialises in child and family issues that may occur after separation and divorce.

Family dispute resolution—a process where a family dispute resolution practitioner assists people to try to resolve some or all of their disputes with each other following separation and/or divorce. (Most people just call this mediation but the government can't resist a good three-letter acronym.)

***Family Law Act 1975* ('the Act' or the Family Law Act)**—the legislation in Australia that covers family law matters.

Family law registry—a public area at a family court and Federal Circuit Court where people can obtain information about the court and its processes and where parties file documents in relation to their case. (Although most documents are now filed electronically on the Commonwealth Courts portal. If you have a lawyer, they will file documents for you.)

Family report—a written assessment (or report) of a family by a family consultant. A report is prepared to assist a court to make a decision in a case about children.

Family violence—violent, threatening or other behaviour by a person that coerces or controls a member of the person's family (the family member), or causes the family member to be fearful. Examples of behaviour that may constitute family violence include (but are not limited to):

- an assault
- a sexual assault or other sexually abusive behaviour
- stalking
- repeated derogatory taunts
- intentionally damaging or destroying property
- intentionally causing death or injury to an animal

- unreasonably denying the family member the financial autonomy that they would otherwise have had
- unreasonably withholding financial support needed to meet the reasonable living expenses of the family member, or their child, at a time when the family member is entirely or predominantly dependent on the person for financial support
- preventing the family member from making or keeping connections with their family, friends or culture
- unlawfully depriving the family member, or any member of the family member's family, of their liberty.

Family violence order—an order (including an interim or temporary order) made under a law of a state or territory to protect a person or persons (including children, if necessary) from family violence. The orders are called different things in different states, as follows:

- New South Wales—apprehended violence orders
- Queensland—protection orders (but commonly referred to as domestic violence orders or DVOs)
- Victoria—personal safety intervention orders
- Tasmania—family violence and restraint orders
- Western Australia—family violence restraining order (FVRO)
- South Australia—intervention orders
- Northern Territory—domestic violence order
- Australian Capital Territory—protection orders (also known as domestic violence orders).

Final order—an order made by a court to bring a case to a close (i.e. the end of your case).

Form—a particular document that must be completed and filed at court. Different forms are used for different family law matters.

Independent children's lawyer—a lawyer appointed by the court and usually paid for by Legal Aid to represent a child's interests in a matter in the Federal Circuit Court or Family Court. The independent children's lawyer will meet with child, if appropriate, and gather evidence by way of subpoenas, family reports and psychiatric assessments. The independent children's lawyer is a party to the matter. Legal Aid will seek a contribution to the costs of the independent children's lawyer from you if you have the means to pay.

Interim hearing—a short defended hearing where witnesses usually do not give evidence. Lawyers (or self-represented litigants) will make submissions where they argue their case and refer the judge to evidence in documents such as affidavits or family reports.

Interim order—an order made by a court until another order or a final order is made.

Judgment—a binding legal decision made by a court after all the evidence is heard. Orders will follow a judgment.

Judicial officer—another word for judge.

Major long-term issues—issues relevant to the care, welfare and development of a child of a long-term nature and include (but are not limited to) issues concerning:

- the child's education (both current and future)
- the child's religious and cultural upbringing
- the child's health
- the child's name
- changes to the child's living arrangements that make it significantly more difficult for the child to spend time with a parent.

Mention—a short hearing at court to show the judge how things are progressing. Less complicated issues could be dealt with by the court during a mention, if there is time.

No contact—no contact of any type as far as is possible, particularly if there is abuse, a history of being on again/ off again, emotional game-playing, or any kind of general nastiness.

Parental responsibility—in relation to a child, means all the duties, powers, responsibilities and authority that, by law, parents have in relation to children.

Parenting plan—a written agreement signed and dated by parents and setting out parenting arrangements for children. It is not approved by or filed with a court and is not legally binding but the court will take notice of it. A parenting plan supersedes an earlier court order.

Party or parties—a person or legal entity, such as a corporation, involved in a court case: for example, the applicant or respondent.

Precedent—a decision made by a judicial officer, which may serve as an example for other cases or orders, unless the judge decides the facts of the case are too different.

Procedural order—an order made by a court of a practical nature. For example, the court may order the parties to attend family dispute resolution.

Reasonable excuse—a judge may find that someone has a reasonable excuse for breaching parenting orders if the person did not understand them, or the person breached the orders because it was necessary to protect the health or safety of a person (whether that person was the person breaching the orders or the child, or someone else entirely). The key word here is 'reasonable', and what might feel reasonable in the middle of a heated argument may not feel so reasonable in the cold hard light of a courtroom when confronted by an angry judge. Get legal advice before taking matters into your own hands.

Registrar—a court lawyer who can do things such as grant divorces, mediate at conciliation conferences, sign consent orders and decide the next step in a case.

Respondent—the person named as a party to a case. A respondent may or may not respond to the orders sought by the applicant, in which case they'll be made on the materials that are supplied (i.e. one side won't tell their side of the story).

Rules—a set of directions that outlines court procedures and guidelines. The rules of the Family Court are the *Family Law Rules 2004* and the rules of the Federal Circuit Court are the *Federal Circuit Court Rules 2001*.

Service—when your documents are filed in court, you have to give a copy to 'the other side' (i.e. your ex), generally at the same time. It's very poor form to 'withhold service' (i.e. not give them over to your ex) and your lawyer will get in big trouble with the judge if they do this.

Subpoena—a document issued by a court, at the request of a party, requiring a person to produce documents and/or give evidence to the court. You learn to spell it by spelling it out sub-po-ena but it's actually pronounced sah-*pee*-na.

Super split—where super is 'split' from one party's super account and put into the other party's super account, either by a superannuation agreement (usually contained in a binding financial agreement) or by court order.

Transcript—a record of the spoken evidence in a court case, which the court reporter types up. All court hearings are recorded, except in uncontested divorce hearings. The court doesn't order transcripts in every case and doesn't provide transcripts to parties. If a party orders a transcript, they will have to pay for it themselves and they are expensive (unless and until you get costs awarded, yay).

Adapted from 'Legal words used in court'—Family Court of Australia
http://www.familycourt.gov.au/wps/wcm/connect/fcoaweb/reports-and-publications/publications/getting-ready-for-court/legal-words-used-in-court.

Resources

Beyondblue: www.beyondblue.org.au; telephone 1300 224 636

Child support: https://www.humanservices.gov.au/individuals/child-support

Department of Human Services: www.dhs.gov.au

Department of Veterans Affairs: www.dva.gov.au; telephone: 1800 555 254

Family Relationship Advice Line: www.familyrelationships.gov.au; telephone 1800 050 321

Headspace: www.headspace.org.au

Kids Helpline: www.kidshelp.com.au; telephone 1800 551 800

LIFELINE—www.lifeline.org.au; telephone 13 11 14

Mensline Australia: www.mensline.org.au; telephone 1300 789 978

Psychology Today: www.PsychologyToday.com

Reach Out: au.reachout.com

Escaping family violence

National Domestic Violence and Sexual Assault Helpline (24 hours): 1800 737 732 or 1800 RESPECT

Law Societies in each state and territory

Law Society of the Australian Capital Territory: www.lawsocact.asn.au

Law Society of New South Wales: www.lawsociety.com.au

Law Society NT: www.lawsocietynt.asn.au

Queensland Law Society: www.qls.com.au

Law Society of South Australia: www.lawsocietysa.asn.au

Law Society of Tasmania: www.taslawsociety.asn.au

Law Institute Victoria: www.liv.asn.au

Law Society of Western Australia: www.lawsocietywa.asn.au

Legal Aid in each state and territory

Legal Aid ACT: http://legalaidact.org.au/

Legal Aid New South Wales: https://www.legalaid.nsw.gov.au/

Northern Territory Legal Aid Commission: https://www.legalaid.nt.gov.au/contact-us/

Legal Aid Queensland: http://www.legalaid.qld.gov.au/Home

Legal Services Commission of South Australia: http://www.lsc.sa.gov.au/

Legal Aid Commission of Tasmania: https://www.legalaid.tas.gov.au/

Victoria Legal Aid: http://www.legalaid.vic.gov.au/

Legal Aid Western Australia: https://www.legalaid.wa.gov.au/Pages/Default.aspx

EXTRA WORKSHEETS

Date:	Date:
Questions for my lawyer at our first conference	**Answers**
1.	
2.	
3.	
4.	
5.	
6.	
7.	
8.	
9.	
10.	

Date:	Date:
Questions for my lawyer about arrangements for our children	**Answers**
1.	
2.	
3.	
4.	
5.	
6.	
7.	
8.	
9.	
10.	

Date:	**Date:**
Questions for my lawyer regarding my property settlement	**Answers**
1.	
2.	
3.	
4.	
5.	
6.	
7.	
8.	
9.	
10.	

Index